SILENT REFUSAL:

ESSAYS ON CONTEMPORARY FEMINIST WRITING

Silent Refusal:

Essays on
Contemporary Feminist Writing

Kristina Marie Darling

Black Ocean
Boston · Chicago

Black Ocean
P.O. Box 52030
Boston, MA 02205
blackocean.org

ISBN: 978-1-939568-41-0

Library of Congress Control Number: 2021946801

FIRST EDITION

TABLE OF CONTENTS

DIFFICULTY, INTIMACY & INVITATION

AN AFTERWORD

INTRODUCTION

LE LIVRE MONSTREUX

"In the beginning are our differences."

—Helene Cixous

In his writings on the experience of cultural otherness, Georges Bataille once observed that the marginalized speaker exists at the periphery of a community, as it cannot be safely contained within or held outside it. Within the context of Bataille's work, otherness is defined as a "separation," a visible rupture between the subject and the society that they inhabit. In such a way, marginalized groups function as a veiled threat to the establishment, a population that cannot be housed within its discourse, and thus kept and controlled. More frequently, though, difference is invoked by those in power as a justification for oppression, a reason for exclusion, and the ongoing marginalization of voices and perspectives.

For many feminist practitioners, the experience of otherness is an inexorable condition of inhabiting language. Each sentence, its clean subject-verb-object constructions, enact a particular kind of logic, a causation rooted firmly in a predominantly male, and predominantly Western, philosophical tradition. In her landmark essay, "The Laugh of the Medusa," Hélène Cixous describes this type of syntax as "marked writing," a toxic masculinity that is exorcised onto language and borne into the realms of art, of storytelling, and the imagination.

It is worth noting that in a language like English, every word is by default masculine. Anglophone writers do not have a designated feminine space, which is in fact a feature of many Romance languages. More and more, female-identifying and non-binary practitioners are using innovative approaches to style and syntax to carve out a uniquely feminine space within a linguistic terrain that is inherently hostile to their voices.

Perhaps, for this reason, found forms, invented forms, hybrid texts, and unclassifiable works are seeing a renaissance in the hands of female-identifying and non-binary writers. More than ever, feminist practitioners are attempting to write outside of, beyond, and against this Cixous's notion of "marked writing," its linear and logical structure, and the undoubtedly narrow philosophical tradition that it takes for granted.

In recent years, this vibrant artistic landscape, populated with multifarious hybrid writing by female-identifying and non-binary authors, has taken a turn for the dense, the difficult, the forbidding, and the inaccessible. In an article in *Map Magazine*, a staff writer observes, "Experimental prose is difficult—challenging in the way that foreign language learning is challenging." This is because the rules of language, its implicit logic, and causal structures, are often reconfigured. As in the work of Lisa Olstein, Sarah Ann Winn, Julia

Story, Laurie Sheck, and many other contemporary experimental writers, the sentences fit together, but the words don't cohere in the way that we think they should. We are offered clean syntactic constructions that resist the implicit logic of grammar.

Disorder begins to inhabit the orderly linguistic structures we once thought we knew.

Though many critics have written on poetry and social justice, few have considered this kind of textual difficulty as a feminist gesture. More often than not, this kind of denseness is seen as a failure—to be understood, to master the forms of discourse, to communicate effectively. Of course, you are likely thinking several things: There is no point in creating a text that is difficult, if not impossible, to understand. If female-identifying and non-binary writers inhabit a marginal space in the literary community, as evidenced annually by the VIDA Count, this aesthetic arguably contributes to the continued relegation of feminist texts to the outermost boundaries of the literary world.

The difficult text constitutes a provocative reversal of power, a show of agency and resistance. The feminist practitioner is no longer the outsider, othered within a linguistic terrain that is hostile to her, but instead, she chooses who is granted access into the imaginative world that she constructs, one dense, impenetrable, labyrinthine paragraph at a time.

Before posing questions about artistic failure,

it is necessary to remember that, as Viet Thanh Nyugen notes in an essay that appeared in the *New York Times*, literature and power cannot be separated. Every gesture, every move we make in language responds to, reacts against, propagates, or internalizes existing structures of control, influence, and authority. The expectation that a text be accessible to readers who situate themselves within a specific artistic school of thought, is yet another manifestation of power and linguistic violence.

In her hybrid text, *The End of the Sentimental Journey*, Sarah Vap calls our attention to the striking similarities in how textual bodies and physical bodies are constructed in language. According to Vap, the difficult text is almost always spoken about as though it were a female body and as though the mostly male readers in the room are entitled to "access" it. As the work unfolds, she situates textual difficulty and easiness on a spectrum, challenging us as her audience to find the sweet spot. She returns again and again to the idea of the "payoff," that abiding belief that a text should give in to the reader, but only after the reader has worked for it awhile.

At the periphery of Vap's text is the question of readerly entitlement. Not all texts are intended for every reader, but instead, might be aimed at underground, non-mainstream, or more specialized audiences. To that end, Vap poses the question, "When someone says a poem is difficult, do they mean that the language of the poem, or the mind of the poem, or the sentiment of the poem is not like *his* or *her* language or mind or sentiments?" A reader that demands that a text perform its meaning in a way that they are accustomed to, that is legible in the eyes of the dominant culture, wields their power in a manner that is linguistically hegemonic, all in the name of "good art." In such a way, all the violence that is suffered by female bodies, and the erasure of non-binary identities, is done again through language, through interpretation, and the orders of power that structure the environments in which we encounter literary works.

With that in mind, a text that denies entry, that frustrates a sense of readerly entitlement, is perhaps the most disruptive of all. The difficult text resists the reading act as a wielding of mastery, and it challenges those who approach interpretation as a show of mastery and dominance. What's more, it enacts and performs a separatist mentality that has surfaced and resurfaced throughout radical political movements.

Though syntax, through the dexterous movement between registers and discourses, and through form, many feminist practitioners are saying, quite simply: This text is not, was never, intended for *him*.

This particular variety of textual difficulty, an inaccessibility that is both artistically competent and politically charged, takes many forms, ranging from narrative obfuscation to formal subversion, and it offers challenges to logic and reasoning, which are implicit in the sentence. In the work of Julia Story, the page becomes a visual field, as the writer highlights the containment of her own voice within a legible form, within the sentence, and within language. Her collection, *Post Moxie*, takes the form of neatly shaped prose boxes, which contain within them labyrinths of intricately and impressively crafted language. Yet inside of each prose box, each cleanly shaped linguistic container, we encounter a provocative fragmentation of meaning as most readers have heretofore envisioned it. "Living on the edges of things and people, my experiences (and even my prayers) can be best documented in fragments," Story herself said. Within the context of *Post Moxie*, this idea of the edge, the periphery, can best be understood as the outermost border of what is intelligible to the reader.

"I'm in my membrane-colored sweater and we watch the swirl of generic birds," she writes. "Tears enter your voice when you tell me how long it's been since you fed them. Grammar is made to house a disintegration of the most familiar ontological categories, ranging from sound to color to the animal world. "Birds" appear as something "generic," mass-produced; the "voice" houses "tear" after "tear," becoming something weighty and tangible, and so on. As the ontological categories begin to disintegrate, the relationship between signifier and signified becomes less clear, as we are no longer sure what these familiar words correspond to in a world outside of language and

Moxie's daring artistic imagination. In such a way, possibility accumulates within the text, each elision, each rupture in the rules of syntax creating a proliferation of richly envisioned meaning.

Story shows us, subtly and skillfully, how grammar, its rules and its logic, limits what is possible within the imagination. Yet this critique is housed within the familiar confines of the sentence. For Story, the work of the poet is to expand what is possible within the boundaries of language, to carve a space for an alternative definition of reason, one that is nonlinear and multifarious in its possibilities. As Vap notes in *The End of the Sentimental Journey*, those whose minds, whose sentiments, and whose languages do not operate in such a way will find the writing "difficult." While I do not mean to negate or deny any reader's primary experience of an experimental text, I am heartened by writers who remind us that there is more than one way to inhabit language and, in doing so, expand our sense of what is possible within it.

Like Story's collection, Laurie Sheck's *A Monster's Notes* explores and upholds obfuscation as a feminist gesture. What is withheld from the reader, both within the narrative and when considering the logic that governs the book, becomes a source of power and agency for the feminist practitioner.

The work's monstrous subject matter offers a wry commentary on the ways we as a culture have conceptualized and continue to limit what is possible for the marginalized voice. "She had given her creature/monster/being books to wander in and learn from," Sheck tells us. Just as the monster exists in the space between ontological categories, the voice of the novel sprawls outside of received, legible, and modest forms of discourse, becoming something unrecognizable. The text performs monstrousness through the vastness of the terrain that it claims, its repertoire of innumerable forms, and textures of language. Of course, this vastness might be construed as difficulty, the physical object that is the book becoming a veritable saint's burden to carry from one place to the next. For Sheck, it is this monstrous impulse that can dismantle all that is problematic with language and its radical confusion and make way for something new. As Sheck herself asks, "Who isn't monsterized."

It is the refusal to speak that is perhaps most monstrous. In much of this intentionally difficult, unabashedly demanding writing by women, the careful withholding of narrative context establishes a power dynamic between the poet and her reader. This hermeneutic miserliness can take many forms, ranging from elided transitions to wholly absent exposition, conceptual leaps, and startling juxtapositions. The result is imaginative work that the poet keeps for herself, and ultimately, denies to her audience. Consequently, these poets redirect the focus of readerly attention. Rather than fixating on the semantic meaning of words and familiar narrative structures, we are made to attend to language in all of its materiality, sonic texture, and complexity.

In an essay called "What Poetry Can Teach Us About Power," Matthew Zapruder observes, "following the suggestions of the material of language, instead of trying to bend it to expressing what we already know, is inherently ethical." It is impossible not to note the irony of an older cis male poet, blessed with the benediction of professional opportunity and visibility, writing an essay like this one (and for *Lit Hub*, of all places). But this line of thinking reveals something of Sheck's intentions, as well as Story's and Vap's as they consider textual difficulty as an aesthetic gesture.

This premise, that it is inherently ethical to push language beyond expressing what we already know, suggests that it is language itself that keeps us trapped in familiar ways of thinking and seeing, forever rearticulating an all-too-predictable causal chain. For these poets, then, obscuring intention becomes a way of defamiliarizing language. As a result, we are rendered suddenly and startlingly aware of our desire for narrative, for continuity, for causation, even more so as they are withheld from us.

And so, the feminist text becomes monstrous, unwieldy, no longer dainty, or well behaved. Its meaning sprawls outside of, and beyond, the familiar structures of meaning-making. Of course, such a text is unlike anything we have seen before, its alterity writ large in the very texture of its language. If we begin to conceptualize difficulty as difference, as a performance of and reaction against being pushed up to the margins, what does that open up within our reading of innovative texts by female-identifying and non-binary authors? After all, the politics of textual difficulty are inextricable from their aesthetics.

Here is a sentence that refuses to make clear its intentions.

Here is a veiled threat, woven into the lining of a white dress.

SILENT REFUSAL

SILENCE AS EMPOWERMENT
AND RESISTANCE

I n *Good and Mad*, Rebecca Traister writes, "On some level, if not intellectual then animal, there has always been an understanding of the power of anger: that as an oppressed majority in the United States, female-identifying and non-binary people have long had within them the potential to rise up in fury, to take over a country in which they've never really been offered their fair or representative stake." As Traister rightly points out, there exists a muted rage among many of us, which eventually surfaces in social media posts, rallies, and other overtly political actions. Yet at the same time, silence proves to be an often-overlooked expression of anger.

In their work, Traci Brimhall and Rebecca Hazelton explore the ways silence and a purposeful withholding of narrative context can have revolutionary implications. Just as Julia Story in *Post Moxie* creates a text that is forbidding in its visual appearance on the page, as well as in its intentionally inscrutable language, these gifted poets create a power dynamic between the artist and their audience, in which the text's silences and elisions become a show of agency for the feminist practitioner. By choosing who has access to the imaginative world they've created, and withholding artistic intent, they ultimately assume a stance of empowerment as they inhabit the predominantly male artistic tradition they have inherited. In such a way, Brimhall and Hazelton offer a provocative reversal of texts by cis white men, in which the same power dynamic cultivated by a purposeful withholding often functions as a mere performance of the status quo.

For Hazelton and Brimhall, this cultivation of mystery—arguably even difficulty—comes through most visibly in their relationship to traditional forms. Brimhall and Hazelton utilize the familiar couplets, tercets, and quatrains of an inherited artistic tradition, Yet they use them to create a provocative reversal of power from within their well-trod structures. In their poems, lyric forms are made suddenly and wonderfully strange by a careful, intentional, and disruptive withholding of narrative context. As Brimhall herself observes, "O mystery. O hopeful stab of joy."

Hazelton's *Gloss* begins with a poem entitled "Group Sex," in which the speaker explains, "There's you and your lover and there's also his idea / of who you are in this moment, and your idea of who / he should be, both of these like both of you but better—". Even in these opening lines, Hazelton establishes a stance of power, which manifests first in her pairing of direct address with the poem's undoubtedly intimate dramatic situation. By excising the narrative scaffolding that normally surrounds a love scene, and beginning in medias res, the poem challenges the reader's likely sense of entitlement to exposition. The poem's use of the second-person amplifies and suits the poem's overt defiance of our belief that a story takes the form of a progression, a gradual and slowly paced dolling out of plot elements.

As the book unfolds, Hazelton invokes couplets, tercets, and the lyric while at the same time assuming power and agency as she decides how much, and how little, the reader is allowed into the imagined terrain she is constructing. She writes in "Love Poem," which takes the shape of pristine tercets:

Sometimes you are the more elegant

of the two cigarettes in the cut-glass ashtray.
Sometimes you are the smoke curling up

in the slow frame rate, cutting to mist

on a dark road rising.

Though offering the illusion of order, Hazelton begins once again in medias res. In doing so, she eschews language in which there exists a clear correlation between the signifier and what is signified. Instead, she chooses what philosopher Paul Ricouer once referred to as the "symbolic" dimension of language, that image or detail that generates meaning and possibility for the work's audience. As the "cigarettes" and their "cut-glass ashtray" multiply in their potential readerly interpretations, Hazelton withholds the authorial guidance that has become all too commonplace in contemporary poetry. Within the confines of seemingly orderly tercets, Hazelton creates a provocative reversal. This critique of a literary form from within its confines in some ways resembles Julia Story's use of the justified prose block to call attention to language as containment, as a kind of violence done to voice and narrative.

Still, Hazelton assures us, "You might be forgiven for thinking there's an order to things." Yet she skillfully challenges the power structures that we have become accustomed to in poetry, in which one caters to an outdated notion of the reader as arbiter, as consumer, rather than an actual constituent of the text. In many ways, this idea of the reader is steeped in a tradition that is less than hospitable to feminist voices. "When he is a woman I feel optimistic," she explains. Hazelton's artful revision of this gendered model of reading opens up the possibility for new ways of interpreting, and relating to, feminist texts. As Hazelton herself asserts, "No cake baked by man from woman born / will small me now."

In turn, Brimhall's *Saudade* offers a narrative in fragments. Like Hazelton, Brimhall purposefully withholds the readerly luxury of exposition, those moments in which the work's connections and confluences are made abundantly clear. Presented as a story told in many voices, it is the space between these character's voices, narratives, and perspectives that becomes charged with possibility. For Brihmall, creating a polyphonic text proves to be an inherently feminist endeavor, as Saudade's myriad silences and elisions challenge her audience's expectations and their beliefs about what the task of reading should look like.

Like Sarah Vap, Brimhall frames the act of interpretation as a patriarchal enterprise, in which the reader strives to attain mastery over a given work. "Perhaps I can control him," Brimhall's speaker conjectures. Indeed, she shows us that the polyphonic text, in its bright apertures and its provocative ruptures, resists a reader's attempt to dominate and colonize the text through their interpretive efforts. In the text's silences, there exists little hermeneutical certainty. "Why not a prophecy and its interpreter instead of angels chaperoning a resurrection?" Brimhall's speaker asks. Here she may very well be reflecting on her own craft, as the book's polyvocal structure cultivates greater freedom for both the poet and her reader.

As she brings together mythology, familial history, and divinatory poetics, Brimhall, like Hazelton, ultimately allows the space words to speak. She writes in "For the Glory," "O heavenly dark rendered in a woman's body. I wake / and find the grave empty. My wife says she is ready / to serve a god instead of a man." What is most striking about these lines is the way that each sentence asks us to take a conceptual leap. Though offering us the semblance of order, these neatly constructed, grammatically faultless sentences contain chasms between them. Much like Hazelton's unconventional use of couplets, tercets, and other familiar forms, Brimhall's adherence to the rules of language ultimately expands what is possible within their strictures. As Brimhall commands the reader, "oh, resist."

If readerly interpretation exists as a wielding of mastery, how can feminist practitioners change these structures of power, claiming some of that agency for themselves? In their innovative feminist texts, Brimhall and Hazelton use silence, rupture, and elision to offer a provocative reversal, deciding for themselves who is allowed into the imaginative terrain they have created and to what extent. Though typically envisioned as a form of oppression, an unwanted destruction of voice and agency, silence is reframed by Hazelton and Brimhall as a source of power, an intentional withholding, and a necessary challenge to a kind of readerly entitlement. As Brimhall observes, "Here's the never of silence, the yes of an idolizing crowd."

RUPTURE & REVOLUTION: ENJAMBMENT IN FEMINIST POETRY

n her study on the philosophy of religion, Pamela Sue Anderson writes, "Beginning with Greek philosophy's equation of the male principle with reason and mind and action, the female principle was left only with a contrasting identification in terms of matter, body and passion, and potency. The subsequent history of Western philosophy, despite major conceptual shifts, displayed a characteristic logic and form." As Anderson rightly observes, much of Western philosophy is predicated on a definition of reason that has over time been coded as male. Yet many readers fail to realize that this limiting definition of reason is embedded—and enacted—within our thinking about language, most of all, within the conventions of grammar. Indeed, each sentence, with its clean subject-verb-object constructions, enacts and performs a very particular kind of causation, which arises out of a philosophical tradition that has undoubtedly been coded as male.

The poetry collections—*A Little More Red Sun on the Human* by Gillian Conoley and *Blood Feather* by Karla Kelsey—invoke enjambment and its ensuing silences as a means to disrupt the syntactic unit as it is presently conceptualized. In doing so, they challenge the causal structure implicit in the familiar rules of grammar. By creating a poetics of rupture and interruption, Conoley and Kelsey dismantle the predominantly male and predominantly Western philosophical tradition that underlies our assumptions about reason, rationality, and sense-making.

In much the same way that Hazelton and Brimhall weaponized silence in their innovative texts, Conoley and Kelsey use enjambment, and the subsequent fracturing of the syntactic unit, to set forth an alternative definition of reason, one that is more hospitable to feminist interpretations of history, culture, and lived experience. Through their provocative use of fragmentation, these forward-thinking poets liberate the mind from a narrow intellectual inheritance in texts that are as philosophically rich as they are conceptually striking.

In her poetry collection, *Blood Feather*, Kelsey writes, "[PART FIRST] in autumn I decided / to cancel desire cancel Eve cancel / Venus cancel elicit meetings with Hadley." Here Kelsey's provocative choices with respect to enjambment— for example, breaking the line after "decided" and after "cancel"—literally halve the clauses contained in this narrative's sentences. Given that these are the opening lines of the collection, the reader is purposefully jarred out of a likely complacency with the structures (and strictures) of language. Yet the reader is made to look again at the words themselves, as these carefully considered enjambments reveal juxtapositions and confluences that are swept away in the logical progression of the sentence. For example, the placement of "desire" and "Eve" in the same poetic line, and the repetition of "cancel" three times within the same measured breath, purposefully undermine the various hierarchies imposed upon language by grammatical convention. In much the same way that tercets and quatrains evoke containment in Hazelton's text, grammar itself appears as a reminder of the ways women and nonbinary people gradually internalize what is essentially a patriarchal logic.

Like Hazelton and Brimhall's purposeful withholding in *Gloss* and *Saudade*, Kelsey's artistic intention is revealed gradually, as her engagement with archival material is brought to the fore. She writes in the book's notes after the three dramatic monologues contained within it have drawn to a close: "From these women and the archives out of which they are created come facts and experiences resonant with the contemporary moment. For example, a 215 BC Roman law forbade women to own more than an ounce of gold, ride in carriages, wear multicolored garments—particularly those trimmed in purple, symbolically male and royal." For Kelsey, giving voice to these archival texts not only suggests or evokes a new grammatical structure, but rather, it warrants one. After all, a new story merits its own vessel, one suited to a revolutionary purpose.

Kelsey writes midway through the collection:

> [...] dust recalls
> fire that edged but never entered
> our garden [PART THIRD] to be
> as wind through a chandelier rustling
>
> burn the ragged muslin edge of
> the curtains and the dress

Here the syntactic unit exists in provocative tension with the poetic line. Reminiscent of feminist texts by Jennifer Militello and Tarfia Faizullah, Kelsey's lineation does violence to the philosophical tradition, as well as the limiting definition of reason that excludes the female-identifying subjects whose voices she exhumes within the archive. Out of this violence, a new kind of logic emerges, a definition of reason in which wind, sound, and "a chandelier" exist in the same rhetorical space without exposition. Indeed, we are made to see the beauty and the possibility inherent in this associative logic, reminiscent of the wild flights of imagination that govern dreams and the submerged continent of the unconscious.

Like the work of Kelsey, Conoley's poems resist a predominantly male definition of reason, logic, and sense-making. Yet Conoley also calls our attention to the ways reason and logic serve a very particular model of reading, in which the act of interpretation is a patriarchal enterprise, manifesting as a visible wielding of mastery, a form of conquest and domination for the reader. For this kind of individual, difference—as it manifests in language—presents a formidable conceptual challenge. This brings to mind the question that Sarah Vap poses in *The End of the Sentimental Journey,* "When someone says that a poem is difficult, does he or she simply mean that the language of the poem, or the mind of the poem, or the sentiment of the poem is not like *his* or *her* language or mind or sentiments?" The unruly music of Conoley's poems, much like the work of Kaveh Akbar and Henk Rossouw, uses fragmentation of the syntactic unit to reframe the task of readerly interpretation. For Conoley, reading becomes an exercise in humility, and in turn, possibility.

Conoley writes in "The Invention of Texas":

The sea left this place

to fend for its own water,
leaving prickly wind

and one yellow color.

Here the relationship between the sentence and the poetic line exists in constant flux. Conoley's lineation at times intersects with the end of syntactic unit, but more often, splices or interrupts it. For example, breaking the line between "place" and "to" offers a much different rhythm and cultivates an indirect or circuitous reading experience, compared to line breaks like: "fend for its own water,/leaving prickly wind." The inherent instability of Conoley's text, in which the logic that governs language is constantly shifting, prompts the reader to assume a more active role, as they negotiate and renegotiate the linguistic terrain they are traversing. Much like Laurie Sheck's sprawling and ambitious archival project, *A Monster's Notes*, Conoley's text proves inherently unstable.

In many ways, it is this instability, cultivated by rupture and interruption, that resists patriarchal models of reading. There is not a single logic that governs Conoley's text, but rather, a multiplicity. As a result, there is no unified key to discerning artistic intention. Conoley asks the reader, like the speaker of "The Big Picture," to "learn to love what's there like a child." In other words, Conoley foregrounds the immediacy of our experience of language, its materiality, through the silence, rupture, and elision that she invites into her poetry. As the book unfolds, we witness Conoley, like the speaker of "Native," "taking the meaning / and giving back the meaning / as the photographs do with the life."

If grammar is in itself a worldview, then how can experimental poetry reveal its inherent subjectivity? Kelsey's *Blood Feather* and Conoley's *A Little More Red Sun* on the Human use silence, rupture, and elision to reveal grammar as one possible way of organizing thought among many. In such a way, they offer a novel variation on Brimhall and Hazelton's reclamation of silence as a form of power in a literary text. For Kelsey and Conoley, the poetic line allows us to see juxtapositions, contrasts, and confluences that are usually borne away in the logical progression of the sentence. Indeed, it is the silence that these writers invite into language that allows us to see its shape more clearly. As Conoley writes, "the door flies open and a road of light falls through it."

"WHAT IS THE WEIGHT OF LIGHT": NOTES ON SILENCE, INTIMACY & THE LYRIC IMAGINATION

In her landmark book, This Sex Which Is Not One, Luce Irigaray begins with the story of a man breaking into a locked house. This anecdote, rich in its theoretical underpinnings, foregrounds the work's concerns with questions of power, intimacy, and the psyche. For Irigaray, these dimly lit rooms, in all of their strangeness and idiosyncrasy, stand in for the space of the imagination. The story, then, becomes one of psychological violence, as the man asserts ownership over the small house without first understanding its architecture or mapping its terrain. What's more, his presence ultimately shapes what is possible in each of the rooms, limiting what can be attained in our dreaming and determining the boundaries of our imaginative work.

In the spirit of Irigaray's unsettling psychological metaphor, nonbinary writer Henry Hoke's *The Book of Endless Sleepovers* and Julia Cohen's *I Was Not Born* react against a long tradition of works that imagine the reader as passive and disempowered, only to be fundamentally changed by myths, images, and narratives they had no agency in creating. By presenting us with work that's as participatory as it is deliberate, Hoke and Cohen posit their writing as a corrective gesture, framing the creative text as a space for readerly collaboration, dialogue, and collective experience.

In the spirit of Irigaray's unsettling psychological metaphor, nonbinary writer Henry Hoke's The Book of Endless Sleepovers and Julia Cohen's I Was Not Born react against a long tradition of works that imagine the reader as passive and disempowered, only to be fundamentally changed by myths, images, and narratives they had no agency in creating. By presenting us with work that's as participatory as it is deliberate, Hoke and Cohen posit their writing as a corrective gesture, framing the creative text as a space for readerly collaboration, dialogue, and collective experience.

In *The Book of Endless Sleepovers*, Hoke uses these carefully framed silences to involve and implicate the reader in the book's portrayals of intimacy. "The water is stupid with stars," he writes in an irreverent reframing of Mark Twain's well-known stories of Tom Sawyer and Huckleberry Finn. Here, Tom wonders if he is in love with Huck, and the reader is prompted to ask whether Huck actively contributes to—and revels in—what is in effect an unequal share of power.

"When the girls twist the stems of apples and the pop-tops of canned Coke they always end up on H for Huck. Never," Hoke explains, "in the history of twisting girls, have they reached the letter T." In many ways, he gestures toward Tom's complicity in this power imbalance, suggesting that agency resides in the creation of narrative. As the book unfolds, Tom ultimately disenfranchises himself through the grandiose and self-effacing stories that he constructs around his interactions with Huck: "Tom always asks the same question: 'What time is it?' And Huck always has the same answer: 'it's a little bit night and a little bit morning.' Tom wakes at this time for the rest of his life."

Yet by framing narrative as the creation of power, Hoke ultimately empowers the reader. It is the space between these prose sections, those bright apertures, that prompt the reader to participate in the process of creating meaning from the text, to actualize the book's imaginative work. Much like Gilian Conoley and Karla Kelsey's provocative use of fragmentation, this book's episodic structure, and its myriad silences and elisions, create a portrayal of intimacy that is as performative and participatory as it is innovative in its use of hybrid forms.

"Imagine yourself on a raft in a slow-moving river at night," Hoke writes, "Every soft animal makes sounds from the bank. You are in the center of the raft, and surrounding you are all your friends, asleep." These brief lapses into the second-person frame the reader as a constant presence within the narrative, an alterity that speaks through the text. Hoke's use of montage similarly creates a space for the reader to breathe into. In this respect, the reader is invited into the various power dynamics of the text, and at same the time, they are invited to change them. There exist as many possible texts as there are readers, and it is this multiplicity that contributes to the work's sense of mystery. As Hoke himself writes, "to find out the secret, knock three times."

Cohen's *I Was Not Born* offers a similar exploration of narrative, agency, and readerly participation. Presented as a series of linked vignettes, which take the form of therapy session transcripts, lineated poetry, flash essays, and hybrid prose, Cohen's approach to style compliments—and complicates—her chosen subject. In much the same way that Hazelton merges postmodern experimentation with received literary forms, Cohen's book is fragmented in its structure, involving and implicating the reader in the impossible task of creating meaning from a tragic experience.

"Born in a deadlight? Stop teasing," Cohen writes, "Furnace full of patient stars. Here because I could not abandon love: coffee grounds, a box of opened cereal, cherry magnets." Here Cohen's wild associative leaps prompt the reader to forge connections among the various ephemera that surrounds the narrator: "coffee grounds," "cereal," "magnets," and of course, "stars." Much like the book's fractured structure, Cohen's dream-logic calls our attention to the conspicuous absence of exposition, reminding us that narrative is how we derive meaning from experience, and it's the stories we tell that make us ourselves. These silences, then, speak to the absence of apparent meaning in the wake of tragedy. Yet at the same time, the reader is reminded of their own expository impulses, particularly as they fail and fail again to create the lovely arc of story.

Reading, then, becomes an exercise in empathy, as Cohen challenges the reader "To hold nothing against nothing. To hold nothing against." Like Hoke's work, *I Was Not Born* calls into question common ideas about the power structures implicit in the act of reading. Here, too, the reader is empowered by the work's various silences and ruptures. Yet at the same time, they are made to see the abject futility of the agency with which they are afforded.

The reader, like Cohen's narrator, falls "out of architecture," finding only "a cut-up star." In her study of grief, Julia Kristeva describes melancholia, that "pathological mourning" originally theorized by Freud, as a loss of language. Without a grammar for our experiences of the world, we lack meaning, cohesion, and purpose. Cohen skillfully involves the reader in this struggle to reenter language, and in doing so, the reader can reclaim the stories that define us.

If a readerly participation requires the writer to relinquish some degree of power, how can one ever trust one's audience? Given Conoley and

Vap's critiques of interpretation as a patriarchal enterprise, the possibility of appropriation emerges as one of the dangers of inviting readerly participation. In Hoke and Cohen's poems, we are offered an opportunity for collaboration that is as deliberately orchestrated as it is rich in imaginative possibility. By carefully guiding the reader's imaginative work, Hoke and Cohen present us with incisive arguments (and counterarguments) about how culture imagines the act of reading. As they renegotiate the power structures implicit in our interactions with literacy works, Hoke and Cohen ultimately offer a textual terrain that is at once performative, participatory, and carefully controlled, gorgeous in both restraint and interpretive richness. It is the silence that allows us to see these possibilities, these bright apertures, in sharper relief. As Cohen reminds us, "We write poems on the whiteboard of a cloud."

SPEECH, SORROW & LABOR: ON THE POETRY OF ANNE BOYER, SUZANNE SCANLON & LISA FAY COUTLEY

Elaine Scarry once observed that "a made object is a projection of the human body." We must remember that much is housed within the walls of the body: the senses, certainly, but also grief, difference, and the various narratives from which they arise. With that in mind, even the most commonplace items are inscribed with history's discontents and inequities, a startling numbness in the fingertips that is inevitably externalized.

Anne Boyer's *Garments Against Women*, Suzanne Scanlon's *Her 37th Year: An Index*, and Lisa Fay Coutley's *Errata* each explore the many ways difference is written onto the body, as well as the objects that surround us, such as "ill-fitting shoes," "flowers carved out of thick glass," "a cracked bowl." In these works, we are presented with a sorrow that is contained in everything we touch, a sorrow that is manifest in the tears of things. They conceptualize a sadness that is at once tangible and historical, a melancholy stitched into the seams of every dress.

Much like the work of Julia Cohen and Gillian Conoley, these books also share a commitment to representing a grief that is uniquely female. The artifacts of femininity offer a point of entry to this consideration of history, sorrow, and its persistent manifestation in the products of our physical and intellectual labor. For Boyer, Scanlon, and Coutley, mourning is present in the making of the very spaces we inhabit and in the decorations mounted in every room of the house.

Anne Boyer's *Garments Against Women* skillfully situates the products of the speaker's labor within a larger economy of texts, knowledge, and goods. As the book unfolds, womanhood is revealed as inextricable from the marginal spaces of a market economy, which is made real by the disparities in how we value different types of labor. The female body is burdened by a system of valuation that is not kind to it. A mounting heap of work and debt wears on the speaker's physical being: first, a "toothache" that she cannot afford to fix, the scent of "ammonia" that lingers in a cheap apartment, and the persistent feeling that her body is "unwell."

For Boyer, each object is not only a projection of the human body, its wellness or lack of rest, but also the body's place in a larger market of labor, goods, and cultural production. These objects, particularly the artifacts of femininity, also become a form of protest. Boyer's descriptions of sewing are especially telling in this regard. She writes, "I could spend a year learning to do well what I have spent twenty years doing badly, and after that year, I could still be bad at what I do." Her narrator abjures our predilection for convenience and reclaims the economic value placed on her time, revealing the clothes she has fabricated herself as an unexpected confluence of feminism, history, and labor rights activism: "Always when I sew I think of Emma Goldman with her sewing machine, or Emma Goldman during her first night in jail 'at least bring me some sewing.'" To stitch a garment by hand is to reclaim agency in a culture that constantly requires her to trade choice for efficiency.

This interest in sewing, its connection to labor that has traditionally been coded as female, is enacted gracefully in the book's larger structure. Although in Boyer's narrative, sewing is often an affirmative choice, there are some things that the speaker of these poems doesn't stitch together. The book is a series of linked prose texts, which move through various psychic landscapes: economic anxieties, transformative experiences of art and literature, and friendships. We transition quickly from the aisles of Target to the "heroic refusal" to participate in this consumer culture. The fragments refuse a narrative arc that would situate meaningful relationships within an economy that is hostile to them. In such a way, the purposeful withholding of narrative context, which one sees in the work of Brimhall and Hazelton, becomes a performative critique of the various economies in which texts circulate.

Boyer elaborates:

> I will leave no memoir, just a bitch's *Maldorer*.
> There's a man. He tells me he does not like the
> version of the story in which he is like Simon
> Legree who ties me down to the railroad tracks.
> This is because he is like Simone Legree who
> ties me down to the railroad tracks.

Here, as in the larger structure of the book, the
absence of narrative implicates a larger capitalistic
system and our expectations as readers. In
her refusal to construct a memoir, we see the
structures of economic power silencing her, and
that quietness arouses only guilt in the reader.
We all participate in and maintain a system that is
persistently unkind to each of us.

Boyer does not have to trace sorrow through the
hand or count each stitch of the dress. We see that
we are already folded in its dark cloth, weighed
down by its seemingly endless embellishments.

Susan Scanlon's collection of marginalia also
interrogates the economies in which objects,
labor, and texts circulate. In much the same way
that Boyer calls our attention to the systematic
placement of women's and nonbinary subjects'
labor on the peripheries of the marketplace, *Her
37th Year: An Index* offers a carefully rendered
account of intellectual and emotional upheaval
that is confined to the marginal spaces of a text:
those small, succinct, and orderly entries in a

book's index. Like Jenny Boully's *The Body: An Essay*, a series of blank pages populated only by footnotes with wildly imaginative content, Scanlon's formal choices immediately evoke the hierarchies of value that we impose upon different types of writing. Similar to Rebecca Hazelton and Traci Brimhall's use of silence to interrogate and reverse a power imbalance between the poet and her reader, Scanlon's marginal text moves from the periphery of our attention to the center and becomes the main text. The textual hierarchy is not only questioned, it is reversed.

The sorrow of inhabiting a marginal space is a kind of affect that is well-documented in feminist writing. It is merely one variety of mourning for voice, agency, and visibility. For Scanlon, form offers an incisive commentary: the narrative, which depicts a female academic whose greatest hopes even she feels are unspeakable, is indexical. Married and at an age where the expectation is stability, she involves herself in an affair with a married writer, of whom we glean only one identifying detail: he is "the man in boots," whose name cannot be spoken, but who soon becomes the absent center of a gorgeously fractured narrative. Scanlon's index, then, is both an enactment of this silencing and a resistance. As the unruly narrative sprawls from one index entry to the next, we are made to see the violence inherent in cataloging language, intellectual labor, and desire. To sort, organize, and assign value is to create a hierarchy, to elevate one thing at the expense of another. In this way, Scanlon's use of marginal forms might be read as a dramatization and performance of the same critique of language and its arbitrary structures that we see in the work of Kelsey and Conoley.

As in Boyer's work, Scanlon's discussion of women's and nonbinary subjects' labor is grounded in familiar objects: "perfume," a "medical bracelet," and a quote from Anais Nin on a "thumbtacked index card." We are reminded that a literary text is also a "made thing," another product to be circulated within a larger economy. For Scanlon, even the failure of "Selective Serotonin Reuptake Inhibitors" and other treatments for depression become the focus of trying intellectual labor, the meticulous cataloging of experiences and things in such a way that they will be legible within the marketplace. In this sense, her particular variety of resistance diverges markedly from Boyer's. Rather than refusing to construct a narrative edifice that conflates the personal and the economic, Scanlon rejects the attempt to render even bodily suffering "useful." Though recounted by a narrator who expresses a fear of "being marked," Scanlon shows how we are all "marked" by our complicity in a system that limits what is possible in language, limits our ability to organize the world around us, and limits the very structure of conscious experience.

Because little is assumed to be at stake in peripheral textual spaces, the margins of a text are rife with possibility. Scanlon writes in her entry on "Exceptions": "as when your husband declares that he loves you but feels three things: bored, lonely, and invisible. Also: he thought this sort of longing, desperation, was only for sad old people." Marriage and one's spouse "declaring that he loves you" is the normative ideal, while an affair is presumed to exist on the perimeter of this supposedly more valuable relationship. Yet this husband, as an "exception," is now confined to the margins of the margins. As Scanlon dismantles the hierarchies we impose upon texts, other hierarchies, of labor and relationship and desire, are inevitably called into question.

Scanlon provocatively situates desire within a discussion of women's and non-binary subjects' labor within the academy. When the narrator of *Her 37th Year* is offered admission to a graduate program that could increase the perceived value of her intellectual labor, it is not her husband but "the man in boots" whom she cannot leave. The economy in which these characters circulate seems to value the wrong texts, the wrong relationships, the wrong desires. Yet an entire infrastructure depends on them—the work of the professoriat outsourced to the precariat.

Much like Scanlon's use of the index and its abecedarian constraints, the poems in Coutley's *Errata* inhabit the inherited and seemingly innocuous forms of a received intellectual economy through couplets, tercets, and quatrains. Though offering us what Helene Cixous once described as "marked writing," Coutley appropriates these familiar structures only to reveal their inherent artifice. While similar in this respect to Hazelton's reclamation of tercets, quatrains, and other inherited literary forms, Coutley ultimately widens the scope of this critique. We are reminded that one renders an orderly account of an experience or a perception so that it may circulate in a marketplace of labor and goods: "Consider the going rate / for hormones, then picture an eager group / of eBay bidders." The impulse to commodify is not limited to material things, but rather, it encompasses affect, the body, and the very words we use to describe them. The strict formal constraints that govern each poem suggest the impossibility of escaping this economy of texts: "Call it a burning building or a sinking ship, / either way you're in it." Coutley asserts in pristine tercets. As the book unfolds, these orderly stanzas, like our systems of valuation, are revealed as yet another form of containment—of voice, of affect, of possibility—for the speakers of these poems.

As in Scanlon's index entries and Boyer's fragments, Coutley's formal choices offer a powerful commentary on content. The seemingly uniform stanzas highlight a persistent desire to impose order on our experience of a disordered world: "Even the dentist is muttering prayers // for the last tooth in his gums, though my father's / certain there's no good reason for such a thing / to be saved. Open a mouth & pull. Done." Here the decay of the human body is ornamented by the work's formal flourishes. Elsewhere, Coutley evokes the myriad ways that the received structures of language, grammar, and narrative are internalized: "even before I learned the word I knew / the shame that came from fearing / fear rooted in the fiction of my mind." Her enjambments, particularly the oddly timed pauses (for example: "fearing/fear"), suggest the speaker's unease inhabiting a linguistic framework that is not her own. Coutley renders us startlingly aware of the flaws of received forms, as well as their undeniable necessity. These familiar structures, after all, make the complexities of inner experience ("fearing/fear") intelligible to the larger world. They allow for dialogue within a community bound together by its shared forms of discourse. In such a way, Coutley engages a question also central to the work of Story, Hazelton, Kelsey, and Conoley, and arrives at the same imperfect conclusion. The feminist writer must work within the containment of grammar and those culturally legible forms of writing and work to expand what is possible from within their confines.

"Each day this year, one of us has declared / some state of emergency," Coutley writes: "a broken wrist, / a faulty video game, an unwashed dish." The state of alarm in each line exists in tension with the pristine tercets that house the narrative, suggesting the precariousness of the various types of order we have come to expect: the routines of domestic life, the wholeness of the body, even the grammar that renders voice and affect intelligible.

Yet any resistance to these received forms, any critique or alternative model, inevitably borrows from the intellectual economies that it dismantles. "Under this influence," Coutley explains, "it will take years to learn she's a room she drags / with her." Language and its accompanying philosophies haunt the speakers of these poems. *Errata* skillfully works within familiar frameworks to expand our sense of what is possible within them. In a house that we are certain is burning, Coutley offers us a "tourniquet," a "suture," and lastly, a "match."

THRESHOLD AND POSSIBILITY: ANNA MOSCHOVAKIS & ALLISON BENIS WHITE

In his study of the work of Walter Benjamin and Freidrich Nietzsche, James McFarland describes silence as the "herald of possibility," suggesting that it represents not an "expressive limitation" but a "commitment to an expressionless ideal." For McFarland, the cultivation of silence within a literary work constitutes a deliberate gesture, one intent on opening up meaning and richness within the text, rather than circumscribing possibility through exposition. Indeed, silence, in all of its indeterminacy and hermeneutic uncertainty, allows a multiplicity—with respect to narrative, interpretation, and readerly experience—to manifest within what was once a one-dimensional rhetorical space.

Allison Benis White's *The Wendys* and Anna Moschovakis's *Eleanor, or, The Rejection of the Progress of Love* do justice to the richness and complexity that silence, in all of its myriad forms, can invite into a literary work. Much like Traci Brimhall's *Saudade*, they employ white space, that bright aperture, to allow multiple narratives to orbit around the same temporal moment, illuminating and complicating one another. For White and

Moschovakis, silences represent a liminal space in which the rules of storytelling no longer hold. In these brief moments of rupture, the narrative and its inevitable interpretation become entirely changeable, subject to radical revision. Like Henry Hoke and Julia Cohen, White and Moschovakis share a commitment to cultivating a layered approach to storytelling, which ultimately becomes a critique of narrative cohesion and its inherent artifice.

With that in mind, their commitment to revealing the artifice—and the inevitability—of narrative comes through most visibly in the use of rupture, elision, and interruption as stylistic gestures. The swift transitions between points of view, narrative strands, and disparate versions of the same events remind us of our own expository impulses, that desire to create unity and cohesion through our participation in the text. Yet at the same time, it is these glorious apertures that allow the narrative to refract and fold back in on itself, as the same experience gives rise to a seemingly infinite array of interpretive possibilities. As White bserves, "So many red feathers in my mind."

Similar in structure to Brimhall's *Saudade*, White's *The Wendys* appears as a series of linked persona-driven poem sequences, unified only by their heroines' first names and untimely deaths. Here, we encounter Wendy Darling, Wendy O. Williams, Wendy Given, Wendy Torrence, and Wendy Coffield, whose redacted narratives inevitably invite our imaginative work. Dedicated to the author's late mother, Wendy, the poems also explore grief as displacement and distraction, tracking the mind's ambulatory restlessness in the wake of tragic loss. As White's speaker explains, "Because it is easier to miss a stranger / with your mother's name, young and doomed."

Much like the provocative enjambments of Kelsey's *Blood Feather* and Conoley's *Selected Poems*, the apertures between White's sections, and between individual lines and poems, functions much like "a constellation of cigarettes in the dark," a space for transformation. "My mind will not cool," White warns us. Indeed, we orbit around the same moment in time, returning again and again to that alluringly absent center. In doing so, we watch the speaker accumulate losses as well as their myriad narrative justifications.

White elaborates in "Zero":

> What is love but our need
> to see another face?
>
> Another body, her long black
> sweater still hanging
> in my closet.
>
> Like the suicide note
> in Japan still carved
> into a tree.

Something to hold
after you read.

Like Brimhall's divinatory poetics, White shows
us the poem as visitation and re-visitation, a
loss suffered over and over again in the mind
and the heart. Here, the speaker returns to the
psychic space into which we were ushered in
prior poems, where "your cool hand [still rests] in
my hand, carved from ivory or ice." Yet it is the
space between poems that allows her to begin
again and again, to layer narrative upon narrative,
reminding us that the past is as multifarious in
its interpretations as it is singular in its temporal
boundaries. The speaker's "need / to see another
face," then, becomes as rich in its imaginative
topography as it is impossible. As White herself
reminds us, "of the four truths, I remember two:
we are alone, we will suffer."

Moschovakis's *Eleanor, or the Rejection of the Progress
of Love*, presents the reader with two distinct
narrative threads—a literary text and its creation.
As the work unfolds, the reader gradually realizes
that writer and heroine are one and the same,
that the work presents fiction as a space in which
the self is seen as other, ultimately made strange
by this critical distance. As Moschovakis herself
observes, "Something has crossed over in me. I
can't go back."

As in White's *The Wendys* and Brimhall's *Saudade*,
it is the interruptions in the text that allow for

a gratifying instability, in which perspective, storyline, and their philosophical underpinnings can suffer provocative reversals. We find ourselves shifting between text and meta-text, between product and process, and between ways of seeing the world. Consider this passage:

> Halfway down the block of her lover's apartment, she was reaching into her bag to feel for her keys. She pulled them out and held them in her fist like a weapon while the top edges of the canvas book bag, too empty with the laptop gone, flapped in the wind.

> Her name is Eleanor. Did you think she didn't have a name?

> ———

> Or do I mean that it had come to create her? Things don't necessarily happen in that order.

Here it is the white space, the apertures between paragraphs and sections, that allow the rules of the text, that familiar contract between reader and author, to shift without warning. As we transition from the "laptop" and its absence, the bag "flapping in the wind," to direct address, we are made to see that the pauses, those bright apertures, are spaces of possibility, transcendence, and change. As in White's hybrid text, this inherent instability allows us to see the same character and the textual landscape that surrounds her, from myriad vantage points, among them metafictional, theoretical, academic, and deeply personal. As Moschovakis herself notes, "His lips had settled into a faraway smile, and I watched him not weep while clearly weeping in his mind. He'd never reminded me so much of Eleanor."

If meaning and narrative multiply in the space between things, how do we know which thread to trace, which one will lead out of the labyrinth of interpretive possibilities? In her experimental novel, Moschovakis states explicitly that "what I want to say is that Eleanor doesn't know." Indeed, choice in both of these texts seems beside the point, as it is their multifariousness that is an integral part of their meaning. This proliferation of storylines, set off by the silences between them, become a commentary on the uselessness—and the undeniable compulsion—of narrative. Yet for White and Moschovakis, it is the bright apertures, those shining thresholds, that allow us some degree of agency in the wake of tragedy, that familiar and necessary freedom to begin again.

WRITING RACE: SILENCE AS PERFORMANCE & READERLY IMPERATIVE

I n an article published in *Political Theory*, Mihaela Mihai argues that in recent years, "complex injustices [have been] passing as 'misfortunes' that nobody feels responsible for." Indeed, this displacement of responsibility has contributed to a culture of passive spectatorship, especially when considering instances of racial injustice. As Mihai rightly insists, a world of binary distinctions—good and evil, just and unjust, victim and perpetrator—allows individuals to overlook larger systemic problems that foster injustice.

At the same time, many writers, like Morgan Parker, Tommy Pico, Anaïs Duplan, and Danez Smith, have been turning to experimental forms as a vehicle for presenting both social criticism and alternative ways seeing, representing, and understanding what Hannah Arendt calls "the active life"—in other words, the spheres of work, citizenship, and political action. These formally innovative texts naturally lend themselves to a complexity that is missing in much of contemporary discourse, while also fostering a more active role on the part of the reader. For these writers, the most effective way to present a new vision of social relations, and the systems of meaning and value operating within society, is to model its workings for the reader—to involve them and implicate them within its structures.

Much like Rebecca Hazelton, trans writer An Duplan has harnessed the power of both poetic tradition and its silences as he offers a vision of a more just society. By drawing inspiration from New York School poets, Frank O'Hara in particular, Duplan brings their distinctive poetic techniques into new sociopolitical territory. By invoking the terse lineation of O'Hara's well-known poems, among them "The Day Lady Died," "Ann Arbor Variations," and "Ave Maria," Duplan creates a provocative relationship between speech and silence. In each of Duplan's collections, the moments of rupture become both an indictment of the reader and a necessary imperative, as we are made suddenly and startlingly aware of the problematic systems in which we think, write, and relate to others.

For Duplan, literary tradition and this kind of systemic injustice are intricately linked. He writes in "A Love Song to Dean Blunt in Three Parts," an essay included in his multi-genre collection *Mount Carmel & the Blood of Parnassus*, "I don't want to give up my body just because it's being read incorrectly by the people around me." Duplan skillfully calls attention to the unfair choices that society's broken power structures force upon historically marginalized groups of people. Further, by presenting this text on black paper, with a white typeface, Duplan evokes the inversion of these same hierarchies through his visual presentation of the work on the printed page. Indeed, to revise our thinking, we must also reimagine the cultural imagination that we have inherited. After all, the construction of a literary cannon, as described by Charles Altieri, is a "manifest power." In many ways, this is the very power that Rebecca Hazelton, Julia Story, and Laurie Sheck claimed for themselves through their approach to poetic craft.

Duplan, in the end, offers a similar reversal from within the confines of a received literary tradition. For example, he writes in "On a Scale of 1-10, How 'Loving' Do You Feel?", from his poetry collection, *Take This Stallion*:

> I don't love Yeezus as much as I love
> Yeezus when I'm with you. And rappers
> get lonely too. Zip-lining is not
> a cure-all. Kim knows that
> and knows how to backwards-
> straddle a bike like a real woman's woman.

Though steeped in postmodern popular culture, the artistic lineage of this text is strikingly clear. Consider O'Hara's well-known poem, "The Day Lady Died":

> I walk up the muggy street beginning to sun
> and have a hamburger and a malted and buy

an ugly NEW WORLD WRITING to see what
the poets
in Ghana are doing these days

Though innovative in its enjambments, most
readers would likely find O'Hara's presentation of
an international literary tradition dated, dismissive,
and problematic. Yet O'Hara's distinctive
lineation, in which the line exists in visible tension
with the sentence, still proves provocative for
contemporary readers. By rupturing the syntactic
unit (for example, "buy/an ugly" and "poets/
in Ghana") O'Hara mirrors the violent impact
of Lady's death on the speaker, evoking both
postmodern experimentation and its discontents.

In "On a Scale of 1-10, How 'Loving Do You Feel?'",
Duplan bears O'Hara's lineation into new and
provocative sociopolitical territory. By placing
the poetic line in tension with the sentence,
Duplan evokes a familiar literary heritage while
also revising it. More specifically, he uses O'Hara's
literary tropes to create a space in which black
popular culture is elevated to the realm of high
art, placed squarely and prominently within a
heretofore mostly white literary cannon.

In much the same way that Conoley used silence
to cultivate a collaborative rapport with her
readership, Duplan's use of enjambment within
this poem, and many others, exudes a similarly
democratic impulse. As each piece unfolds, the
unusually timed enjambments remind us of the

violence implicit in being made to inhabit a tradition that is hostile to one's voice, aesthetic, and identity. Duplan capitalizes on our culture's general discomfort with silence, anticipating that the reader will eagerly attempt to fill these spaces with narrative. In such a way, Duplan reminds us of the choices we are faced with in engaging with any cultural text: to what extent does our participation become an act of erasure? Can we reimagine speech as a kind of radical listening?

For Duplan, part of conversation is leaving room for the other to speak, a goal that he achieves with each enjambed line, each moment of rupture within the text. In such a way, the silences within *Take This Stallion* and *Mount Carmel & the Blood of Parnassus* become both cultural critique and readerly imperative. Duplan skillfully models radical listening in the relationship he cultivates between the text and its audience, prompting us to reimagine our interactions with artistic tradition and our lives in language.

Later in "On a Scale of 1-10, How 'Loving Do You Feel?", Duplan writes:

> There is so much you don't know
> about me. I once met an Australian,
> told him he could have my underwear.
> He didn't want it. I'm better
> when I'm mysterious.
> I'm better when I've had a few

days to forget
how much I want you
to want me like you want Kim.

Here, Duplan uses each line break, and each oddly timed silence, to cultivate what Mary Kinzie referred to in *A Poet's Guide to Poetry* as "half-meaning." This gesture proves especially visible in Duplan's choice to break the line after "you don't know," and, similarly, "I'm better." As readers, we wait in suspense to see how the clause will end. After all, most of us have been acculturated to crave wholeness, cohesion, and the resolution of narrative tensions. The moments of silence become liminal spaces, where a transformation of meaning—and the logic that governs the poem—become wholly possible. The fact that Duplan cultivates liminal spaces within the sentences is perhaps most provocative of all. The sentence, and the predominantly Western, predominantly male, definition of reason and causation that it represents, is promptly destabilized.

In such a way, the radical listening that Duplan requires of us as readers asks us to suspend the prevailing models for organizing and structuring experience to allow room for alternatives to be proposed. The space of the poem, then, becomes a hypothetical testing ground for new ways of imagining social relations and the communities borne out of them. Duplan writes in "On a Scale of 1-10, How 'Loving Do You Feel?":

White people like to ask me about my hair.
They say did you get a haircut. I say no
it's the shrinkage. 'White people.'

Don't be so pessimistic.
Don't be so sensitive.
Don't go so slow do it faster
nevermind let me do it flip over.

Here, Duplan moves provocatively between two
types of lineation: enjambed lines and lines that
end at the same time as the relevant syntactic unit.
What's particularly revealing is the fact that the
moments of rupture come when the speaker of the
poem is addressing the "white people" who appear
as a collective throughout the poem. The lineation
becomes a powerful social critique, calling our
attention to the ways the speaker's voice and
narrative are cut short, redacted.

Yet at the same time, this poem is rife with
possibility. By the end of the quoted passage, the
unusually timed enjambments become a space
for transformation, where the rules laid out in
the previous lines no longer hold. "Do it faster /
nevermind let me do it flip it over," Duplan writes,
his speaker reclaiming agency within the liminal
space of the line break and its dangerous and
brooding silence.

If the tradition we have inherited is "manifest
power," how does a poet working within its
confines become a pillar of the resistance? In
a promising body of work, Duplan offers us a
tentative hypothesis, calling our attention to the

apertures, the liminal spaces where the rules of language no longer hold. Culling inspiration from his literary predecessors, Duplan uses familiar New York School tropes to cultivate silence within his poetry, and in doing so, creates liminal spaces where anything becomes possible. Here, in these moments of rupture and elision, the rules of society—and the language that structures our relationships—can be wholly transformed.

RADICAL LISTENING:
ON TEXTS BY ILYA KAMINSKY &
DONNA STONECIPHER

n his essay, "Silence," Chris P. Miller asserts that "silence is a chronology, a beginning collapsed into the end." For Miller, silence manifests as the first—and truest—form of compression, a charged and dense rhetorical space in which even time folds in on itself. Susan Sontag describes this remarkable compression not as a destructive force, but rather, as transcendence, a sure sign of language sublimating into dream, insight, and artistic vision. Approached with these ideas in mind, the gaps between words, lines, stanzas, and prose paragraphs become charged with possibility, a liminal space in which the rules governing speech no longer hold.

Like *The Wendys* and *Eleanor, or, The Rejection of the Progress of Love*, Donna Stoncepher's *Transaction Histories* and Ilya Kaminsky's *Deaf Republic* both frame silence not as failure, but as potentiality, transformation, and resistance. In their poems, they invite absence, which manifests at turns as fragmentation, omission, wild and unexplained juxtapositions of images, and a careful withholding of narrative context. Yet in both of these volumes, the reader witnesses silence transforming from elegy to paean to metaphor and back again, as the space between words is made to hold entire worlds.

Though vastly different in style and scope, their poems, through their innumerable ruptures and elisions, frame listening, especially in a rhetorical space characterized by absence, as a radical and visionary practice. What's more, through an undoubtedly performative approach to language, Stonecipher and Kaminsky involve the reader in a deft performance of this soothsaying, this gradual process of divination and revelation. Each collection, then, reads as a ledger of a consciousness transformed by deep listening. As Stonecipher writes, "Aftermath after aftermath after aftermath. Each word was a vault containing the pale blue glass of its history."

Similar in structure to Julia Story's *Post Moxie*, Stonecipher's *Transaction Histories* appear as a series of thematically linked prose vignettes. Yet in the early pages of this collection, the dense, ornately worded paragraphs are perhaps most startling in their fragmentation, as a visible rupture tears at the very center of each piece, its music interrupted, literally halved, by this destructive gesture. Yet this negative space at the very heart of each poem functions much like the "skeleton key" that appears throughout the work, offering a point of entry into the work's potentialities if the reader is attentive enough to unlock them.

"[T]here were locks upon locks in rows," Stonecipher writes, "as in a locksmith's dream, and one key so slippery it kept falling out of her hand into the sky, floating up into the deeps." In much the same way, the intent behind Stonecipher's dense and baroquely lyrical prose constructions seems at first to be elusive. Yet this same certainty often eludes the speaker of the poems herself, as her mind orbits from "the past with its black perfect perfections, its ashtrays and princess telephones" back to the imperfect present as the "glass" falls from her hand shatters "on the balcony." Much like Julia Cohen's participatory depiction of her narrator's grief in *I Was Not Born*, *Transaction Histories* invites the reader to search along with the speaker, for patterns, convergences, and confluences in the vast sprawling texts of time, history, and culture. The elisions in the very center of each poem, then, offer a space for meaning to accumulate, to take hold in the seemingly random fabric of shared consciousness.

We come to realize, along with the speaker, that "What's past is never past, but moves from room to room in the blue honeycomb of the brain, or blooms in domes that crown the fretted space of her thinking." Fittingly, as the sequence unfolds across time and history, these gaps disappear from the book's pages, as a gorgeously fractured narrative arc begins to emerge. Just as in Traci Brimhall's *Saudade*, a transient unity of time, voice, and self is visibly performed in the visual presentation of the work on the page. Similar to Brimhall's polyphonic structure, in Stonecipher's work it is the space between each prose vignette, each intricately imagined possible world, that allows us to see the work's myriad potentialities, selves, and fictive topographies in sharper relief. As Stonecipher herself observes, "as soon as the man came around the café in the evening shilling newspapers, then we remembered that our little world was only one of a profusion of worlds—a single bubble clinging to the great foam."

Kaminsky's *Deaf Republic*, like Stonecipher's *Transaction Histories*, engages white space, silence, and rupture as stylistic devices and extended metaphors. Presented as a dramatic play-in-verse, the stunning poems in this volume frequently end not with a final line, but instead with dictionary entries, translating spoken words into an invented lexicon of sign language. In such a way, the poems transcend speech, just as Stonecipher's prose paragraphs embrace elision and rupture if only for possibility to accumulate within their luminous architectures. Like Rebecca Hazelton's provocative withholding of narrative context, *Deaf Republic* frames silence as not only secrecy, but agency, hope, and resistance.

"*You are alive*," Kaminsky writes, "*therefore something in you listens.*" As the book unfolds, this rapt attentiveness is revealed as the most easily forgotten lesson of poetry in a postmodern political landscape. In some ways resembling the participatory works of Hoke and Duplan, the dramatic verse of *Deaf Republic* actively involves the reader in this reframing of listening as prayer, as invocation, revolution, and inevitable transformation. The reader's knowledge of

Kaminsky's partial deafness renders this gesture all the more powerful, manifesting as part elegy and part intervention.

He writes, for example, in "Deafness, an Insurgency, Begins":

"Our hearing doesn't weaken, but something silent in us strengthens.

After curfew, families of the arrested hang homemade puppets out of their windows. The streets empty but for the squeaks of strings and the tap, tap, against the buildings, of wooden fists and feet.

In the ears of the town, snow falls."

Here Kaminsky uses caesura and careful pacing to evoke the concept described by Miller, of time as chronology, a beginning collapsed into an end. As this piece unfolds, the end-stopped stanzas become charged with tension, as though each rupture signified both the accumulation of history and its eventual undoing. Within the world of these poems, silence becomes both a foreshadowing and an appeal, as these gaps leave room for the reader to participate in the poems' revolutionary politics.

Like Stonecipher's *Transaction Histories, Deaf Republic* reframes silence as possibility, as loss and its inevitable transformation. As Kaminsky himself observes, "silence moves us to speak."

RADICAL LISTENING

SILENCE, DIFFICULTY &
THE POSSIBILITY OF
TRANSCENDENCE:
EILEEN G'SELL, RAJIV MOHABIR
& JULIE MARIE WADE

In "The Metaphysics of Youth," Walter Benjamin observes that "[c]onversation strives toward silence, and the listener is really the silent partner. The speaker receives meaning from them; the silent one is the unappropriated source of meaning." In other words, it is the space between words that sets off language, the dim background against which light becomes visible. For Benjamin, silence was the precondition for a community out of which story arises, and the vast expanse waiting just beyond its inevitable end.

Eileen G'Sell's *Life After Rugby*, Rajiv Mohabir's *The Taxidermist's Cut*, and Julie Marie Wade's *When I Was Straight* each consider, albeit from vastly different conceptual vantage points, the ways silence makes possible our experience of beauty, that "gift of dark lace" woven into each poem. For G'Sell, Mojabir, and Wade, the possibility of transcendence resides in the space between things, and it is always a bright aperture that gives rise to a "queer flutter that knocks about your ribs." These three books share an investment in allowing opulence to be complemented by the reader's own unspoken imaginative work and contemplation, offering us only "the sound of boots through snow and the dark."

Considered together, these writers offer a full range of approaches to what silence can do. In G'Sell's dense, image-driven lyrics, this purposeful withholding often takes the form of absent narrative scaffolding. What is left unsaid becomes an invitation to the reader, a pathway into the book's rich fictive terrain. For Mohabir and Wade, however, each aperture manifests as a kind of rupture, a subtle violence done to voice and language. As Mohabir himself tells us, "Every time you speak they hear a different hell."

In G'Sell's *Life After Rugby*, each line is gratifyingly dense in its presentation of images, types of rhetoric, and vibrant soundscapes. For G'Sell, this disconcerting proximity—of images, lexicons, and narratives—gives rise to countless elisions, as the relationships, the rules that govern this imaginative topography, are often left to the reader's imagination. Indeed, we are offered "a cheekbone shyly brushing your wrist," though the speakers of these poems rarely tell us to whom a body, or an encounter, belongs.

Silence is intricately linked to pacing in G'Sell's work, as the speed with which we transition does not afford time or space for exposition. It is the breathlessness of each poem, their restless movements, and their dense, complex music, that allow silence to inhabit them so fully. After all, the relationships, associations, and resonances, are too numerous to count. Reminiscent of Joshua Clover's *The Totality for Kids* and Kathleen Peirce's *The Ardors*, G'Sell's poems also confront, through their satisfyingly dense constructions and their quick, unpredictable leaps, our own discomfort with silence, while at the same time gesturing at its inevitability. G'Sell elaborates:

> With the best of her Sugar Ray Leonard bob,
> She weaved beyond traffic.
> Symphony, prosperity, the loose mares of time.
> Homily of hominy, the long dreams and lime.
> Outside her glowing loungecar, igloos in space.

In many ways, these lines might be read as an *ars poetica*, as G'Sell gestures at the work's own "symphony" of disparate images, lexicons, and miniature soundscapes. In passages like this one, the reader begins to see that the poems are constructed against silence, but also that the poems exist because of that negative space. It is the absence of narrative scaffolding and all that is left unsaid that allows the story to grow wilder.

Mohabir's poetry reads as a novel take on G'Sell's exploration of silence, elision, and readerly unease. While formally diverse, spanning tercets, couplets, and hybrid experiments, *The Taxidermist's Cut* is

67

unified by an exploration of silence as a kind of violence, a rupture in the faultlessly woven tapestry of voice, narrative, and community. Mohabir writes, "Knowledge / of Violence: / where welts rose on my legs / from the riding crop hidden / by your headboard, / the crumble of song / shuddered in my hands." Here, lineation and its ensuing pauses exist in tension with the sentence as well as with the syntactic unit. Clauses (like "knowledge of violence" and "hidden by your headboard") are halved by Mohabir's deft and provocative lineation. When read through the lens of the book's exploration of cultural otherness, these stylistic gestures take on a new and conceptually arresting significance as Mohabir shows us that silence—in poetry, culture, and our own consciousness—is politically charged. Mohabir offers a degree of self-awareness and reflection that is rare in poetry by cis male white writers that makes use of similar stylistic devices. Instead of using silence to uphold the status quo, Mohabir weaponizes silence in the service of social change.

Mohabir shows us the myriad ways that censorship and the fear, deeply rooted in our culture, of confronting difficult questions, is gradually internalized, shaping one's conscious experience even in solitude. This, Mohabir shows us, is the ultimate form of violence and intrusion. He elaborates:

Your parents are at Bible study, leaving you alone
with the devil inside.
Your clothes are strewn about the floor.
The rain ricochets drops through the windowpane.
Your drops drone and soar from the opened window
as cicadas.
Inside you rain. You are a forgery. Not a wolf. Not an
Indian. Not a son.

What is particularly revealing in this passage is Mohabir's skillful use of caesura. Here, the work's meaningfully timed pauses, the persistent stop and start, give rise to uneasy, hesitant music (most visible in phrases like "as cicadas. Inside you rain."). We are shown that the voice of culture (which manifests powerfully in lines like "You are a forgery.") ultimately engenders silence, even in the speaker's uncontested solitude. Yet at the same time, Mohabir calls our attention to the music that silence allows us to hear. Much like Ilya Kaminsky, he reminds us of the persistence of voice, and of music, even as the voice of the establishment "drones" through "the opened window."

Like Mohabir and G'Sell, Wade's poetry exists at the interstices of speech, silence, and unease. Presented as a book-length exploration of the speaker's life before she came out as a lesbian, the poems in this collection are haunted by a kind of shadow story, a narrative that resides just beneath the surface of these lively, jocular poems. As in G'Sell's poetry, these pieces exist against silence and the confrontation—with selfhood, identity, and desire—that inevitably ensues.

Each of Wade's poems becomes a poignant dramatization of what's left unsaid. As in the poetry of Karla Kelsey and Gillian Conoley, speech calls attention to its own artifice. Wade's poems are constantly gesturing, at turns playfully, knowingly, and sorrowfully, toward all that cannot, will not, be spoken aloud. "I could tell my mother how / I wanted her to brush my hair / & braid it through with ribbons," Wade writes. "I could tell my father how / I loved baking cookies & / pinning damp clothes on the line." Here, what's perhaps most revealing is the line break and ensuing pause before "pinning damp clothes on the line." The moments of elision, as in Mojabir's work, become politically charged, as Wade's speaker struggles to signify and perform an identity that is foreign to her. Through her silence, the speaker also experiences herself as foreign, and this, for Wade, is violence.

Yet she also shows us silence as agency, as a manipulation of a cultural system and readerly expectations. "I might have smiled more then," Wade writes, "the part of my lips so often mistaken / for happiness. In fact, it was something else— // a fissure, a break in the line—the way / a paragraph will sometimes falter / until you recognize its promise as // a poem." In much the same way that Wade's speaker masquerades in her interactions with others, the moments of rupture and elision within the poem ultimately toy with the reader's preconceived ideas about how a narrative should or ought to unfold. Here the pause, that subtle and playful rupture before "a poem," the subsequent delay before narrative resolution, exemplifies the ways silence in Wade's work gives rise to suspense, surprise, and wonder.

Indeed, that speechlessness engendered by culture is appropriated and recontextualized in a way that empowers the speaker, rather than censoring her. Like Mohabir and G'Sell, Wade shows us that each moment of elision contains multitudes. It is in these liminal spaces—the glowing aperture, the tentative sigh, the pause for breath—that the rules of language no longer hold, and anything becomes possible.

"SPARE THIS BODY, SET FIRE TO ANOTHER": KAVEH AKBAR, BRENNA WOMER & HENK ROSSOUW

In the one volume of writing that he published during his lifetime, Ludwig Wittgenstein claimed that "the limits of my language are the limits of my world." Indeed, grammar, and the rules that govern speech acts, inevitably structure our relationships, determining what can—and what may never—be said between two people. Even in solitude, it is linguistic convention that circumscribes the boundaries of our dreaming, even as we begin to sense that bright expanse that lies just beyond our reach.

Kaveh Akbar's *Calling a Wolf a Wolf*, Brenna Womer's *Atypical Cells of Undermined Significance*, and Henk Rossouw's *Xamissa* share a commitment to making audible that which lies at the outermost periphery of language. These writers turn to experimental forms as a means of critiquing of linguistic convention, calling attention to its arbitrary limitations. Indeed, theirs is a critique that performs and dramatizes its grievances with respect to grammar, and we watch as that "whole paradisal bouquet spins apart."

What is perhaps most striking about these writers' experimentation is the way their fractured forms invite silence into the work. As each of these three collections unfolds, we watch as moments of rupture, elision, and interruption gesture at all that lies beyond the printed page. Akbar, Wommer, and Rossouw show us that "we are forever folding into the night," and they give us, through their bold experimentation, a vocabulary for articulating its "regret," "its spiritual conditions," and "its diamonds."

Akbar's *Calling a Wolf a Wolf* is structured as a series of linked persona-driven pieces, many of which make expert use of white space within the line. As the book unfolds, these seemingly small gaps within the text proper accrue vast, wide-ranging, and unwieldly emotional resonances. "As long as earth continues / its stony breathing, I will breathe," the speaker tells us. And in much the same way that Akbar makes us attend to the almost imperceptible rhythms of the physical body, he calls our attention to the space between words, suggesting that the very foundation—of meaning, of speech, of communication—resides there.

When we first encounter silence in the work, it is in the first moments of the opening piece, "Wild Pear Tree." Here, the poetic line is halved, a gap manifesting in the very center, its form making visible all that is yet unspeakable: "It's been January for months in both directions frost." What's perhaps most revealing about this passage is Akbar's use of white space to amplify the limitations of the language we do encounter. Here, we sense a sorrow just beyond the pristine imagery that we are given. It is the sorrow that cannot yet be named that finds a name over the course of the book-length sequence. In these opening lines, however, all that is at that moment unspeakable—addiction, longing, excess and its disappointments—is rendered as a startling absence and that elision is what gives rise to the wonderfully imperfect and awe-stricken music of these poems.

Silence becomes the driving force of the work, the language merely orbiting around its alluringly absent center. Akbar writes, for example:

they all feel it afterwards the others dream

of rain their pupils boil the light black candles
 and pray the only prayer they know *oh lord*
spare this body   *set fire to another*

Here Akbar invokes silence as a way of performing and dramatizing time, both literal time and lyric time, and that temporality is measured in emotional, visceral, and psychic duration. It is the sense that time has elapsed ("they all feel it afterwards") that changes our encounter with the words that do exist on the printed page. But also, it is this sense of time passing that signals all that has been elided by the narrative itself. Here past and present are juxtaposed, and it is the reader's task to create the lovely narrative arc that lends meaning, unity, and form to experience. By gesturing at the arbitrary nature of language, narrative, and their repertoire of forms, Akbar opens up the possibility of alternative models for structuring lived experience. And by the final lines of the poem, we are given one in the *deus ex machina* that inhabits the final line: "s*pare this body set fire to another.*"

If narrative is a kind of conjuring, an appeal for meaning, structure, or order that may not be immediately apparent, language is the space in which that alterity makes itself known. The meaning that we arrive at through the unwieldy apparatus of grammar is indeed an otherness, a specter that haunts a room that is not its own. What's more, it is the space between words where the ghosts of "corpses" and "chariots," the "blank easels" and "orchids" of memory, actually live, waiting for a body to breathe into.

Like Akbar's *Calling a Wolf a Wolf,* Womer's *Atypical Cells of Undetermined Significance* explores how silence, rupture, and elision call into question all that resides on the printed page. She takes physical illness and medical trauma as her subject, interrogating the body as a discursive construction, knowable only through our relationship to language. In much the same way that Akbar forces the reader to attend to the space that separates words and the almost imperceptible rhythms of the human body, Womer calls our attention to the transitions between the many discrete episodes that comprise the book. As in the poetry of Scanlon and Boyer, liminal textual spaces are rife with possibility. For Womer, the female body resides in these apertures, in that bright and liminal place between the various narratives and myths that have been imposed from without.

Presented as an extended sequence of hybrid texts, which shift rapidly between "psychic injury," "emotional shock," and "Lipton iced tea powder mix," Womer's writing mirrors the experience of being a patient through the behavior of its language. She actively involves the reader in the struggle to glean meaning in the space between fractured, contradictory, and ultimately incommensurable fragments of text. Womer writes, for example, in "When a Psychic Says We're Soul Mates":

> Recall how you know the heart,
> and remember the future, the
> brain, the chronic hunger and
> burn; life in a wet summer, loud
> and close---eternal, intolerable.
>
> Number the young.

After this lyrical meditation on the delights and displeasures of the human body, Womer transitions to a prose vignette:

> We drove in the day before Hurricane Isabel with our lives blocking the rear view of our Ford Expedition. There was no available housing.

In the moment between sections—that brief pause—the body shifts from being a site of pleasure (and emotional labor) to a site of endangerment and finally, disconnect, as the speaker manifests as a split subject (with their lives "blocking the rear view" mirror). Indeed, she dissociates from her physical body, giving voice to a palpable separation. The swift movement between "Hurricane Isabel," "crumbling red brick," and "1970s standards" performs and enacts this disconnect, involving the reader in an impossible task of meaning-making and creating unity from a discontinuous experience. "I found a pair of seagulls caught on two hooks of the same iridescent lure," she writes. Here, imagery mirrors the book's philosophical underpinnings.

As we traverse the "trauma," "fatal diseases," and "deal-breakers" that comprise the narrative, Womer shows us that none of these lexicons renders experience more faithfully than the last. Not the "chronic hunger" of the lyric interludes, nor the "categories" articulated in the more scientifically minded sections. Like Akbar, Womer uses silence, rupture, and elision to call into question, and provocatively undermine, what is on the printed page.

Using the same stylistic repertoire, she gestures at the artifice of many conceptual models for understanding the physical body. Much like Akbar's provocative consideration of narrative and syntax, this argument is made through form and technique, rather than in the text proper. As Womer's hybrid sequence progresses, we are made to confront the varying levels of authority and credibility that we attribute to different registers and discourses, which, in this case, range from poetic imagery to medical jargon ("150 viruses, each assigned its own number").

"I wanted to be a mother but only on Sundays," Womer tells us. Throughout the collection, lyrical interludes like this one are juxtaposed with medical documents, patient questionnaires, and records of the senses. By transitioning between rhetorical modes in such a way, Womer suggests that the female voice is rarely accepted as a source of knowledge about the body or a credible vehicle for an explanatory model. Indeed, Womer implies that facts about the body are often only seen as credible when they arrive in familiar forms, particularly those that populate the medical field and the biosciences. Yet it is in the silences and the elisions that these power dynamics become clear to the reader. It is in the apertures that the ethics of the text crystalize. As Womer tells us, "You didn't ask for a *miracle*, but got one anyway."

Rossouw's *Xamissa* continues Akbar's and Womer's exploration of what silence makes possible when articulating a philosophy of language. In the work's "Proloog," he notes that the title of this thought-provoking volume actually derives from linguistic accident:

Perhaps it was here the urban legend emerged: "Camissa," we thought, meant "place of sweet waters" in the indigenous Khoe language. And the waters the urban legend speaks of have run from Table Mountain to the sea, under the city itself, since before the Dutch ships. An untrammeled toponym, from before the 1652 arrival of the Vereenigde Oostindische Compagnie (VOC), "Camissa" became a wellspring for the cultural reclamation I witnessed in newly democratic Cape Town. In the 2000s, Café Camissa shut down to make way for a real estate agency—a symptom.

Here meaning and the task of translating seem straightforward, but begin to unravel and refract over the course of Rossouw's introductory narrative. This anecdote frames the work, as the style of the writing performs this unraveling of narrative continuity.

Like Hazelton's *Gloss*, the book begins with the semblance of wholeness. Yet the reader is borne from pristine prose paragraphs to the almost tangible documents of an archive. We are presented with the author's identity documents and no accompanying information or caption. In an instant, the rhetorical situation of the work changes—the reader shifts from a passive recipient of meaning to an active agent in creating meaning. With that in mind, the space between texts and episodes in *Xamissa* is especially powerful. It is in these bright apertures, the liminal spaces within the text, that the laws of grammar, syntax, and narrative no longer hold. In these brief pauses, the rules of the text and the rules governing its language and narrative can be entirely reconfigured.

"Heretofore unseen:/ a piece of census again/or a ship's manifest/ redacted with ash and/doubt," Rossouw writes. Like many passages in *Xamissa*, even the poetic line serves to amplify uncertainty. Just as the pause before "doubt" conveys even the narrator's trepidation, it is the silences in this work that are made to house the weight of history. Much like Akbar, Rossouw envisions silence as the center around which the book's poetics orbit. Just as *Calling a Wolf a Wolf* creates music out of all that cannot, and will not, be said aloud, *Xamissa* envisions the space between languages, histories, and temporal moments as an invitation, that "half-light" beckoning the reader inside what had once been a darkened room.

As the book unfolds, its form—and the silences to which this experimentation gives rise— becomes unruly, even disruptive, when considering the narrative conventions engaged by Akbar and Womer. Here, we are made to walk through the archive that accompanies any subject's life in language. Handwritten ledgers, official documents, and watermarks are juxtaposed with lines of poetry and lyric fragments. "I write the debris number C 2449 on the form/in pencil and wait for the ash in the half-light," Rossouw's speaker tells us.

In many ways, it is this movement between documents, "secrets," and "fire" that presents such a provocative challenge to what does exist on the printed page. Indeed, the transitions between different types of language and the silence that fills the moments we spend in these liminal textual spaces allow the reader to fully inhabit the archive in all of its indeterminacy, rather than a neatly structured master narrative. In other words, we encounter language—and the histories contained within it—in a non-hierarchical way. Like Womer's interrogation of medical jargon and the rhetoric of diagnosis, Rossouw erases the judgments, and the arbitrary valuations, that we impose upon different types of language and text. What's left is a "field on fire," a subversion of the politics surrounding the very documents he has gathered.

If silence is a gradual undoing, then the space between things makes visible that unraveling. It is the pauses between words that are most dangerous, as they hold the power to destabilize the text that surrounds them. Indeed, Rossouw's archival poetics, like Karla Kelsey's *Blood Feather*, reads as both homage and destruction, a lyric appreciation of the work silence can do (and undo).

When silence becomes a gradual undoing, an unraveling of certainty, there is a violence done by saying nothing. Womer, Akbar, and Rossouw undoubtedly destabilize many of the rules that govern our lives in language. At the same time, they do so with a true ethical sensibility, as their efforts to interrogate, and undermine, linguistic convention are born out of a desire for a way of communicating that's more just and more true. As in the work of Wade, Duhamel, and Mohabir, silence becomes a form of resistance, as well as a weapon and a relic of all that is holy. By interrogating the space between things, these poets have offered a philosophy of language where anything becomes possible. After all, it is in the liminal spaces that rules no longer hold. It is in the brief pauses between arias that it becomes possible to shift keys. As Rossouw observes in *Xamissa*, "I listen not in silence but in song, a form of interruption."

POSSIBILITY IN THE MARGINS: JULIE MARIE WADE, SARAH MANGUSO & MAGGIE NELSON

From the very beginning, we as readers have been conditioned to focus on the words that appear on the page, their semantic meaning, and the larger architecture of plot and theme to which they give rise. It is not often that writers ask us to look away from the text proper, to consider what is possible within the margins of a literary work, or even within the small spaces between the words themselves. Yet there are some exemplary hybrid texts that envision this negative space as an opportunity to leave some things unsaid within the work, suggesting possibilities more powerfully than narrative ever could. Julie Marie Wade's *Wishbone: A Memoir in Fractures*, Sarah Manguso's *The Guardians: An Elegy for a Friend*, and Maggie Nelson's *The Argonauts* each utilize negative space in a slightly different way, but to similar ends, allowing these silences to speak as vitally as the words themselves. What's more, the gaps in their texts no longer signify absence, but rather, they allow us to see the narrative in sharper relief.

And when the story becomes dark, these small apertures begin to let the light through.

Similar to Julie Marie Wade's *When I Was Straight* in its questioning of gender binaries, Julie Marie Wade's *Wishbone* describes, through sudden leaps in temporality, the anatomy of a wedding gone terribly (and inevitably) wrong. The bride leaves her groom standing at the altar, all of the other men waiting in their tuxes, the women inpatient in their hats and gloves. Much like Stonecipher's elliptical *Transaction Histories*, Wade's narrative circles around this alluringly absent center, all the while weaving together vastly different registers and rhetorical modes. Through family histories, letters, lines of poetry, and dictionary definitions, Wade skillfully calls our attention to the ways that language and rhetoric have limited what is possible within our thinking about femininity.

Yet it is what happens in the space between the various components of this linguistic and temporal collage that is most vital to the impact of the book. In a recent interview, John D'Agata explains that lyric essays often "depend on gaps. . . . [they are] suggestive rather than exhaustive." This notion of silence as suggestion and possibility, rather than absence, is useful for approaching Wade's sudden shifts in time, narrative, and register within this collection. Throughout the first chapter, for example, she juxtaposes lines of verse with narrative prose, creating a provocative tension between interior and exterior, memory and actuality, self and world. Consider this passage:

Her fear palpable, the nuggets of her knuckles chattered.

If only we hadn't eaten so much fish...The mercury you know, the madness.
If only we hadn't sent you to Catholic school...Too much time unsupervised with the Sisters.
If only... If only...

Here Wade offers a shift between not only fact and conjecture, but also, between interior ("*If only... If only...*") and exterior ("the nuggets of her knuckles chattered..."). The white space between them, of course, suggests disparity, the impossibility of reconciling one's inner life with what one must present to the world. At the same time, the leap that Wade makes here also implies proximity, the porous nature of the boundaries between thought, and more visible expressions of emotion. In much the same way, we are made to witness "fear" made "palpable," Wade traces the origins of this bodily trembling and "chattering," using this moment of rupture to show that one's innermost experiences almost always manifest in the body's tremulous movements. What's more, the aperture in the text, the gap immediately before the interior monologue is revealed ("*If only... If only...*") becomes a liminal space, in which the relationship between affect and the observable world, and between self and other, is entirely subject to change. In such a way, Wade offers novel variations on the way writers like White, Maschovakis, and Scanlon have questioned textual hierarchies, reminding us that the liminal textual spaces are rife with possibility.

As Wade's book unfolds, the reader is borne from inner experience to the immediately observable, but also, back and forth in time. Here, too, the ruptures between narratives, between moments in Wade's personal history, are liminal spaces. Just as the relationship between affect and the body, between interior and exterior, are subject to revision in these apertures, the terms of lyric address are revealed as entirely changeable. In many ways, it is this shifting between forms of address, and between selves, that is most telling. For example, Wade writes at the very end of her essay, "Meditation 26,"

> My mother took off her sunglasses, wiped them dry. She stood in the gold light, facing my direction. It was then I began to raise my hand, as if to wave, as if to urge her on. But something stopped me. Something hard and unwilling in me froze. I started through the window, cheeks wet with tears. How to say this—we saw each other, we did not see each other.

Wade continues to explore the myriad ways that affect manifests in the body. In much the same way that fear shows through in the previously cited passage, we are made to observe the narrator halting, for reasons that have not yet even surfaced in her consciousness. Yet we are also shown a very particular mode of description in which the exterior is treated as symptomatic, a point of entry to knowledge about the subject's innermost experiences. As we cross the threshold to the next essay, the epistemological approach taken in the previous passage is called into question by an older, more aware self. She writes in the opening paragraph of the next essay:

Love ° in ° a ° Mist

(Nigella damascene) Annual garden flower. Delicate blossoms, usually blue and white. "Self-sows" regularly. Once established, it can be difficult to remove. Common name derives from the nestling of flowering buds in lacy involucre...

Here the exterior is no longer symptomatic of one's interior life, but rather, all the world is a projection. Through careful juxtaposition, Wade makes clear the parallels between the life of the flower and the narrator's own situation, suggesting that one chooses to describe certain phenomena and to recount particular details of an experience, for a reason, which one may or may not be fully aware of. Wade deftly conveys these ambitious epistemological claims not through exposition, but rather, through her use of tone and juxtaposition. By pairing this seemingly detached botanical writing with the subjective prose of the previous section, we are made to see the impossibility of escaping our own consciousness. Indeed, this movement between personal narrative and a detached and clinical botanist's notebook suggests not incommensurability, but rather, proximity.

In Sarah Manguso's *The Guardians*, negative space offers a similar paradox, its opportunities for imaginative work often suggesting proximity between ideas, or at least the semblance of closeness. Like Julia Cohen's elliptical exploration of grief in *I Was Not Born*, Manguso recounts the death of a close friend by suicide, following grief on its tangential orbits through time, space, and narrative. Presented in a series of discrete prose episodes, the work also bears the reader across various rhetorical modes, ranging from the sublime to the journalistic. Rarely does Manguso forge connections between them, but rather, she uses these shifts in tone to create startling and provocative juxtapositions. Like Wade, Manguso uses these moments of rupture to suggest, to invite, and to implicate. Yet her approach is distinctive in that she uses the white space between episodes, and between shifts in voice, to enact and complicate the task of the elegy. The small gaps in the narrative become the place where memory lives and the reader is frequently involved in sustaining and tending to that memory.

Consider this passage:

He liked whitefish. He liked drinking Manhattans.

He timed his jump in front of the train, and that's the end of the story.

The space between sentences proves to be nearly as meaningful as the words themselves. As Manguso offers us disparate and disconnected facts (for example: "He liked whitefish" and "He liked drinking Manhattans"), the aperture between them becomes an invitation, a doorway through which the reader is beckoned. We are prompted to reconcile these seemingly random, and at times disconnected, pieces of information. Over and over again, the reader inevitably fails at this task. Like Cohen, Manguso charges us with work that is ultimately as impossible as it is unforgiving.

And so, the apparent proximity between these disparate pieces of language (for example: "He liked drinking Manhattans" and "He timed his jump...") is revealed as an illusion, a seemingly small distance that it is impossible to traverse. The style of the writing itself becomes a metaphor for grief. As the reader tries and tries again to imagine the person who could house these dissimilar truths and experiences, she is made to grieve with the narrator, particularly as she, too, is faced with the insurmountable task of making meaning and weaving narrative from perceptions, memories, and experiences that are impossible to reconcile with one another.

The reader is made to see the simultaneous inevitability and impossibility of creating narrative from tragedy, of imagining meaning and design in one's most difficult experiences. It is this thematic concern that drives the larger structure of the book. As Manguso shifts from one discrete episode to the next, little is offered by way of transition, a strategy that ultimately implicates the reader in this persistent desire for a master narrative of one's experiences. We are rendered suddenly and painfully aware of our own expository impulses. Manguso writes:

> During our first year together, after every quarrel, my husband and I examined and speculated on the relationships of people we knew, describing lovingly to each other their myriad flaws. Now we're almost able to see our own.

*

> Exactly one year after Harris's funeral, on the elevated track the wrong train screamed murderously by and didn't stop.

Manguso creates a purposeful disconnect, the seeming disparity between sections serving as a metaphor for the ambulatory nature of grief. In much the same way that the narrative wanders through various buildings and corridors, Manguso implies that grief itself is impossible to track in its movement through the various facets of a life. Grief not only gives rise to narrative, but it is woven into the stories of love, acceptance, and human connection that form the very core of one's identity. By transitioning so quickly from a discussion of marriage to the very scene of her friend's death by suicide, Manguso calls our attention to the ease with which grief infiltrates our existence in other narratives, other houses, other rooms. The journalistic style of the second section, with its tone of detached observation, suggests the inevitability of this movement of mourning into other seemingly unrelated aspects of one's life. Grief and its elliptical orbits become pure fact, rather than remaining in the realm of the subjective.

Like Wade and Manguso, Maggie Nelson uses negative space and rupture to explore the nature of memory, consciousness, and the self. The book narrates Nelson's marriage to artist and transgender activist Harry Dodge, remaining firmly grounded in postmodern theory all the while. Frequently eschewing formal citations in passages that engage the work of other thinkers and critics, Nelson instead mentions their names in the margins of the text. The reader is left to consider which observations are being credited to others and to extricate Nelson's response. Yet one soon discovers the impossibility of this task as thought itself takes the form of a conversation. In many ways, the marginal spaces of the book become a metaphor for the self as socially constructed, a locus for found text, appropriated material, and the detritus of culture. We are made to see, through Nelson's use of negative space, the ever-porous nature of the boundaries between self and other.

Nelson writes, for instance:

I collect these moments. I know they hold a key. It doesn't matter to me if the key must remain perched in a lock, incipient.

And in the margins, we see: "*Naomi Ginsburg, to Allen.*" The intellectual tradition we have inherited hovers persistently around the narrator's most intimate experiences. Even when alone, she is part of an ongoing conversation, a dialogue with the various literary and cultural texts she has encountered. The citation's ambiguity, then, proves to be purposeful, as it becomes impossible to extricate self from other, subject from object, viewer from viewed. What's more, Nelson does not convey this idea through the content of the work, but rather, allows negative space to make this ambitious argument about the nature of the self.

In many ways, it is the space between the citation and the text proper that is the most thought-provoking. Nelson seems at first to reaffirm the boundaries between self and other. The literary and cultural texts that she cites are always at some degree of remove, held at arm's length from the narrator's innermost experiences. Yet Nelson constantly calls our attention to the artifice of these supposed boundaries, reminding us that the space between self and other, the aperture that divides subject from object, is merely an illusion. Though seeming at first separate to be texts, entirely disconnected from one another, one observes the myriad ways that Naomi Ginsburg's words (the key that appears in her personal correspondence with Allen, which is later transposed to a passage in "Kaddish") offer the narrator a vehicle for conveying her own affect and experiences. Even more important, the fact that this same image travels from correspondence to poem to lyric essay suggests that all of consciousness is communal, every thought an act of theft.

With that in mind, the white space, the separation between thought and other is revealed as merely a material boundary, which does not extend to thought or conscious experience. Throughout *The Argonauts*, citation and the space that separates it from the text serve a similar function, calling our attention to boundaries, only to reveal them as illusory, imagined, conjectural. It is the space between words that makes this argument, frequently complicating the narrative, while also allowing us to see its shape more clearly.

GRAMMAR: A GAME

think like a bird building nests,
think like a cloud, like
the roots of the dwarf birch

The quadrants must be crisp. Smoothing you into the
long crease of a crane's neck—everything implicit in the
fastening.

I've come to believe that nearly everyone
has experienced grammar in this way—as a
"smoothing," or a "fastening" into place. Sensations
are given form and structure, made to fit within the
"quadrants" of language. At first, we barely notice
the small things that won't acquiesce to grammar:
the physical body, its internal logic, the way that
time doubles back on itself. These absences aren't
felt, since there is no longer a way to express such
longing. The little red books they place in front
of us, with their endless charts and diagrams, have
begun to arrange the world around us, piece by
piece. The order is all we can see.

*

I think of some way of describing it uniquely and then
I go through, so to speak, a sort of
mental ceremony

How does one speak outside the confines of

grammar, without performing the familiar "ceremony" of creating order and coherence? Many women and non-binary writers express disdain for received linguistic structures but fear they will be rendered intelligible without them. For me, this is a uniquely feminist concern, as grammar itself represents a way of organizing the world, an array of hierarchies, not all of which are entirely reasonable or fair. It is gendered pronouns that take precedence over the nonspecific ones, active constructions that are privileged over passive ones. The sentence itself strives for order, logic, clarity of relationships. Indeed, one might argue that language itself, in all of its beauty, embodies what we would classify as "masculine" values. Reason, orderliness, and the mind take precedence over the body. Many women have claimed that the materiality of our being represents an opportunity to forge a new logic, a new order, a new grammar, one that remains separate from the "marked" writing of an unjust society. But where to begin?

*

apricot trees exist, apricot trees exist

Poetry in recent (and not so recent) years has seen numerous attempts to answer this same question: Where does writing the body, where does this new order, this new grammar, begin? Texts by Inger Christensen, Hanna Andrews, and Thalia Field (in collaboration with Abigail Lang) present compelling (and often vastly different) answers.

For Andrews, it is sound, and the materiality of language itself, that we frequently overlook in search of seemingly logical connections between ideas. Andrews turns to the sonic qualities of language as a source of unity, coherence, and structure within her collection. Field and Lang, on the other hand, invoke the inimitable Gertrude Stein, dismantling the boundaries between texts, voices, and languages, suggesting that a language that is truly conducive to creativity is one stripped of hierarchies. Lastly, Inger Christensen seeks to question and subvert grammar from within its entrenched order. Without grammar, some would say there is no language. In these recent books, we see that without grammar, there is no absence, but rather, possibility.

*

The lines we draw and redraw

What survives

Hanna Andrews's *Slope Move* begins by creating a semblance of order. Grammatically impeccable clauses, one after the other: "The fast car is the thing we will not speak," "The morning orange juice glass, cleared," and so on. Within this seemingly ordered syntax, however, one struggles to discern semantic meaning in the traditional sense. As the collection unfolds, one realizes that there is another definition of meaning that's been privileged. Meaning resides not in the relationship between signifier and signified but within the sonic qualities of the words themselves. We are made to experience the materiality of each line, offering us stanzas that crack, sizzle, and hum.

Where does meaning reside, then? In experience, perhaps? Or has meaning been eschewed in favor of language's more experiential qualities? For Andrews, meaning emerges when one creates relationships between phenomena. What's intriguing about the poems in *Slope Move* is that these relationships need not be made to fit within any preconceived conceptual framework. Rather, they emerge organically as she utilizes the repetition of sounds to forge connections between disparate images, ideas, and types of language. She writes, "Color clusters, spontaneous blooms: the lit match that completes the metaphor, his ghost with pale carnation hands. As storybook, the chrono-halt is elegant: a thematic connect-the-dots..." Here Andrews's alliteration ("color clusters") and assonance ("spontaneous blooms") creates a sense of unity among images that might not be so easily matched using conventional subject-verb-object constructions. What's interesting about passages like this one is Andrews's self-reflexivity. She takes pride in the fact that she calls upon her reader to "connect the dots," to learn a new way of inhabiting language, a way of understanding language through sound and the senses.

*

Throughout Thalia Field and Abigail Lang's collaboration, *A Prank of Georges*, readers encounter language in all of its instability and equivocation. The meaning that arises organically through sound, the relationships that surface as a result of alliteration, assonance, and consonance, proves slippery, deceptive even. In many ways, *A Prank of Georges* reads as an engagement with (and interrogation of) poets like Andrews, who privilege the sonic qualities of language over semantic meaning.

What emerges, then, from this cross-examination? Field and Lang note the many pragmatic functions for which language must be useful. Not all language can or should circumvent logic, grammar, or reason. Through their choice of title, the coauthors evoke George W. Bush, a figure who haunts the manuscript, noting that repetition (of sounds, of names) created an artificial sense of continuity between the former president and his predecessor. Repetition becomes, within the political realm, a way of maintaining an unacceptable status quo, one more way of creating legacy and privilege.

As the collection unfolds, Field and Lang pair this cautionary gesture with a playful dissolution of boundaries between languages, rhetorics, and registers. Here we see language stripped of its hierarchies, and it is this linguistic environment that proves most conducive to creativity. While critiquing the use of poetic logic in the political realm, this same associative logic proves engaging when utilized in the proper context. The co-authors elaborate, "Very frequently alights on the trunks of trees. Having remained in a distended state for a short time, it generally expels the air and water with considerable force from the bronchial apertures and mouth.." While such fragmentation and humor would have little use in a political debate, the collaborators suggest that within the proper context, linguistic play can be a powerful vehicle for change. Fragmentation, juxtaposition, and the mixing of registers make possible an insightful critique of language that claims objectivity, suggesting that this clinical rhetoric remains as subjective as the French poetry with which it is juxtaposed. For Field and Lang, there is no flawless mode of representation, but linguistic games that are played, particularly when mixing and matching rhetorical modes.

*

in mid-November, a season
when all human dreams are the same,
a uniform, blotted out history
like that of a sun-dried stone

Inger Christensen's *Alphabet*, too, confronts the reader with the dangers inherent in linguistic games. The book uses parallel grammatical structures (particularly subject-verb-object constructions) to present phenomena as varied as one can imagine: "doves," "dreamers," and "dolls." As these vastly different ideas and images are made to inhabit the same linguistic structure, Christensen prompts the reader to consider the ways that grammar homogenizes thought. To what extent, she asks, do vastly different ideas, dissimilar images, and sensory perceptions, call for their own distinct modes of representation?

What's perhaps most interesting about *Alphabet* is that this critique emerges from within the confines of grammar. Indeed, the book retains an abecedarian structure throughout. Why, one might ask, does Christensen present these ideas within a homogenizing, stifling grammatical system? One might argue that Christensen acknowledges both the perils and the possibilities of grammar. Just as language, and the structure we give it, risks homogenizing thought and expression, it creates community by giving individuals common ground. This idea comes through most powerfully in the disparate images that are gracefully unified by the book's parallel constructions: "lightning and wheat," "tears," "autumn marked for death."

Perhaps one might read Christensen as presenting not an entirely new grammar, as we see in Andrews, but rather, a call for innovation within grammar. While acknowledging the dangers inherent in the linguistic games depicted in Field and Lang's collaboration, Christensen highlights the necessity of grammar for creating and maintaining social relations, as well as collaboration. For Christensen, the task is not to invent a new grammar, but to expand what is possible within it. And in *Alphabet*, we are presented with the world.

ice ages exist,
ice of polar seas, kingfishers' ice;
cicadas exist, chicory, chromium
and chrome yellow irises

DIFFICULTY, INTIMACY & INVITATION

UNFATHOMABLE DISTANCE: JENNIFER S. CHENG, ROCHELLE HURT & KAREN VOLKMAN

E MANUEL LEVINAS ARGUED that intimacy takes us from the impossible, to the infinite, and back again. In this interstitial space, we are transfixed by the boundlessness of another consciousness—a luminous, intricate, self-contained world that is ultimately inaccessible. Yet this vastness continues to reveal itself, offering glimpses of a psychic terrain that lies just beyond what one can know.

Jennifer S. Cheng's *House A*, Rochelle Hurt's *In Which I Play the Runaway*, and Karen Volkman's *Whereso* offer constructions of intimacy that fully and convincingly acknowledge this complexity. Through their novel and provocative variations on traditional lyric address, these poets reveal closeness as a kind of "corporeal speech" that forever equivocates. In each collection, we are asked to consider, albeit through a slightly different conceptual lens, our eternal alterity, that all-too-familiar condition of "wanting the world through a window," as Hurt describes it.

With that in mind, the presentation of the "you" is perhaps most telling in these finely crafted book-length sequences. The love object is both a "cross-section of water," impossible to render, and a gravitational pull. We are made to see the allure (and the impossibility) of a sustained, meaningful moment of recognition, that "faraway hour" when both the "I" and the "you" fully reveal themselves to one another. Each poem, and the silences that accompany them, remind us that someone else's mind is like an ocean, "fluid and wafting in refracted light." What's more, these poets know that despite this persistent "unmooring," this "willful" and "soundless" distancing, "the body will blur its boundary, will embrace."

Cheng observes, in an essay on craft published in *The Black Warrior Review*, that every story of intimacy is haunted by "a shadow story." For Cheng, this hidden narrative is almost always the history of language itself. *House A* shows us the "chaos and wholeness" of a voice that is sedimented with its own past, even in the most personal moments of lyric address. Indeed, the speaker's lexicon is revealed as being at once mediated and insular, a social construct that ultimately isolates. "We each live within our own language," Cheng explains, and any closeness, any true connection requires "stitching these languages together." Yet speech is not as simple as the relationship between signifier and signified. Rather, Cheng reminds us that the larger structures of power and authority that surround us are embedded, and enacted, within our smallest grammatical choices. "And how relieved I was," she writes, "no longer to be embarrassed by my mother's voice but to feel her broken sounds again as intimacy, as home." Here, we are othered by and through language, as each inflection, each "folktale" slowly reveals an "anchoring of place." After all, it is an individual's movement through language that allows us to situate them amidst the inevitably contested borders and territories that make up a larger body politic. Language, for Cheng, is an *"inhabited surface*, like the wooden grain surrounding an embedded nail."

It is perhaps for these reasons that Cheng's book begins by depicting an impossible intimacy. Presented as an epistolary exchange, "Letters to Mao" allows us to witness the "man of history we know so well" being presented with the speaker's most private familial exchanges. In much the same way that language (and its political implications) infiltrate the farthest corners of the mind, Mao is shown the "the dark silhouette of a mother's hair," "the dust and corners" of a home. Any intimacy is revealed as both deeply personal and inevitably collective, as it is mediated by a shared historical imagination.

Indeed, the closeness that Cheng's speaker cultivates—whether through lyric address, memory, or the creation of narrative—is persistently intruded upon. As the sequence unfolds, a "mother's off-key lullabies" and even "the movement of a body in sleep" become an "island that wasn't even yours." Cheng writes, for instance:

> Dear Mao,
> I want to describe for you the watery life of home, and by that I do not mean the ambiguity of homeland. For homeland is something embalmed in someone else's memory, or it is a symbol, both close to the heart and a stranger you reach for in the middle of the night

Here the lyric becomes a performance of what has been lost, becomes elegy, and finally, becomes an impossibility. By entering language, we have surrendered an essential part of ourselves, and as a result, we have given over our ability to share that "small" and "tunneling" space with another. Yet Cheng upholds the possibility of compassion and connection, even in a divisive, sometimes hostile cultural landscape. Although the speaker's "homeland" is described as an "ambiguity," and the recipient of this deeply personal letter is a mere "symbol," both are still held "close to the heart." Fittingly, the voice of empire never speaks back, but rather, becomes a conduit for "the biography of the collective," a "spreading of constellations across a dark chart."

Rochelle Hurt's first collection, *The Rusted City*, is marked by a decidedly polyphonic approach to both narrative and the lyric. Reminiscent of Virginia Woolf's *The Waves*, Hurt shows us that the creation of any story is a shared endeavor, as each "wife," each "quiet mother" takes turns describing the "impatient decay" that surrounds her. Hurt's latest book, *In Which I Play the Runaway*, returns to this enduring interest in collective consciousness, while also bringing her multi-voiced lyricism to bear on concerns that only occupied the periphery of her earlier work.

Hurt's second collection, much like Cheng's *House A*, considers the ways intimacy is mediated by a shared cultural imagination. A fugitive speaker drifts between personae and voices, among them "Aunt Em," "Dorothy," and "The Lone Ranger." In this sequence, any semblance of empathy, love, or understanding is buried, "splintered with shreds / of unfamiliar syllables," beneath a heaping accumulation of received narratives.

"The sky behind you," she writes, "is a sherbet pastiche of movie set hues." Here the narratives that connect us, making possible shared experience and culture, are also an intrusion into the most intimate parts of the psyche. Hurt shows us that the stories and archetypes that provide frameworks for our thinking, that build community across geographic and temporal boundaries, are also a subtle and deeply unsettling presence in what we once thought were private exchanges. As "silence blooms" between the speaker of these gorgeous poems and her absent beloved(s), we see her unmoored by the very characters she aspires to, who ultimately keep her "houseless" and "husbandless."

Like Cheng, she shows us the lyric "I" as inevitably collective, undoubtedly mediated. What distinguishes Hurt's collection, however, is her unflinching presentation of her speaker's "breaking" and "slippery" psyche. Because of this proliferation of narrative—that "empty grave" of postmodern culture—the "I" is persistently drifting, ambulatory. "I fall in love with surfaces," Hurt writes. She elucidates for us, bravely and strikingly, that the depth of emotion, the "honeymoon" to which every film and novel aspires, has become an impossibility, an indistinct and beautiful memory, "a perpetual past tense" that haunts the luminous, vast, "brimming" mass media circulating around us.

Much like Volkman's previous collections, *Whereso* situates the individual voice within a linguistic landscape that is temporally bound and sedimented with history. We are made to see, whether in the Petrarchan sonnets of *Nomina*, or hybrid prose of *Spar*, the ways that received forms of discourse structure our most private interactions. Yet *Whereso* also explores the agency of the individual in language, the myriad ways that "the throat-flute uttering its constant note" offers a kind of subtle resistance.

For Volkman, it is the intrusion of language, this ever-present strangeness within the self, that makes intimacy possible. Like Cheng and Hurt, she fully acknowledges the ways that the mind is mediated by grammar and culture. Yet she shows us, deftly and compellingly, that these received narratives can be fractured, "collapsed into particles," remade entirely. It is through this cracked lens, this "totality of pieces," that we come to know and truly understand the other. For Volkman, the inevitable "levitation into clarity" cannot be anything other than mediated, as it is this commonality, this "bridge," that "makes the force containable," that gives us language and structure for our experiences.

In this collection of intricately linked poems, Volkman offers a lyric "I" that is at once fragmented and charged with desire. "A contour of relation," she writes, "swells, hurls." It is no coincidence that many of these poems take place in the old world, replete with "pageant," inhabited by a speaker who "loves" these monuments and ruins "as material." Here, intimacy is none other than an encounter with cultural memory, "needle-bright and bleeding," as it is made and unmade by another consciousness. This unequivocal embrace of intimacy as mediation—and desire as only possible because it is bounded by time and history—most distinguishes Volkman's poems from those of Cheng and Hurt.

As *Whereso* unfolds, this "retrouvé of the past-pulse" is enacted in the very texture of the language itself, offering a vision of the lyric that is as polyphonic and historically sedimented as it is electric. She writes in "Stranger Report":

no gesture
can arrest
crawling or leaping
both are a deeping

of traceable action, intentions on a stage. We
are your auditors, calculating ruptures, in the
invisible lines determining

movement as pattern, this precision beyond a
norm.

Here the lyric "I" arises from a confluence of
vastly different lexicons and registers. As in the
polyphonic texts of Eileen G'Sell and Julia Story,
the language of business ("traceable action," "we are
your auditors") collides beautifully and seamlessly
with academic diction ("calculating rupture") and
everyday speech ("this precision beyond a norm").
Volkman asks us to consider, through her careful
juxtapositions, voice as a social construct, all of
thought as a collective endeavor, even when one
believes one is alone. *Whereso* is filled with gorgeous
poems like this one, which show us, strikingly and
effortlessly, that it is "the textures and tinctures"
of received culture that allow us to truly appreciate
the other, because they prompt us to speak and—
finally, inevitably—be understood.

If intimacy is both an impossible desire and
infinite possibility, lyric address may very well be
an attempt to think through this contradiction.

In these volumes of poetry, one encounters this paradox in all of its beauty and complexity. Here, we are offered a carefully constructed philosophy of interpersonal connection, which is at once boundless and bound by the realities of human consciousness. In such a way, Volkman, Cheng, and Hurt exploit the same tension between individual and collective, and between freedom and tradition, that we see in the work of poets like Karla Kelsey, Gillian Conoley, and Julia Story.

Yet it is through their innovative constructions of poetic voice, their polyphonic and formally dexterous approach to the lyric, that we begin to recognize the constant presence of the other within the self. Whether offering a lyric "I" that is multi-voiced or a "you" who exists as inaccessible radiance, these poets show us intimacy as mediated, and mediation as a kind of intimacy in itself. We are never alone with the other because we are never alone with ourselves.

"MY HEART PEDALS SHUT": ON DISTANCE, DESIRE, AND LYRIC ADDRESS IN RECENT POETRY

In much of contemporary experimental writing, there is a tendency to valorize fragmented approaches to the lyric, to praise the disintegration of voice. This approach is filled with risks, among them a troubling lack of clarity in the terms of address. More often than not, the intimacy that is at stake between characters in a poem, the inevitably intriguing relationship between the "I" and the "you," remains poorly articulated. We are left with the mere promise of plot, a gesture toward persona and voice, the luminous fragments of so many plausible narratives.

With that said, Emma Bolden's *The Sad Epistles* and Megan Kaminski's *Desiring Map* are rare exceptions to this disconcerting trend in poetry. These writers offer innovative variations on traditional lyric address that are as carefully considered as they are contemplative, reminding us that the precision with which the "you" is defined does not foreclose artistic or imaginative possibility.

Though presenting us with clearly delineated

rhetorical situations, a multiplicity is still housed within each seemingly simple manifestation of the love object. This expertly orchestrated complexity is brought to bear on incisive discussions of love, loss, and longing. In each of these finely crafted collections, the "you" becomes an accumulation—of memories, of dreams, of experiences—and each utterance of the unadorned pronoun gestures toward the very impossibility of signification. Bolden and Kaminski engage a rich tradition of lyric address while at the same time interrogating it, each poem a reflection on the philosophical problems inherent in its own making.

Throughout *The Sad Epistles*, Bolden's language orbits around an alluringly absent center. "I'm flayed, a waiting," she explains. The "you" is known to the reader only through the speaker's desire, a longing housed within every darkened "hallway," the room she inhabits "hung" with "ghosts." Presented as a series of epistolary fragments that document a long-distance relationship, the poems in this chapbook offer a syntax shattered by an unfulfilled wish. "People are liars. // Petals are fingernails. // I am liar for saying so," Bolden writes. These rhythmically obstructive pauses and the declarative structure of every sentence convey the power that the love object wields over the speaker. Stammering and uncertain, she is rendered nearly speechless in his absence.

As in the hybrid texts of Julia Cohen, we pass through the ruination he has left behind—"a soot bird," "a sooty porch rail"—and gradually discern what is at stake in this exchange of letters: He may bear the speaker into a more vibrant linguistic landscape, or pull her out of language entirely. In *Black Sun*, Julia Kristeva describes mourning as "loss of speech." Words no longer cohere when placed side by side, and the meaning that was once found there becomes an impossibility. *The Sad Epistles* enacts this idea through its fragmented form, its resistance to narrative, and its eschewing of musicality in the conventional sense. Consider this passage:

> Your jaw is an opening I like too much, the back of you heel one I sing to.
> If I were an egg I'd peel myself.
> If I were an egg I'd strip
>
> To talk being the most difficult
>
> To scalpel my own To flay

Like Cohen, Bolden unequivocally asserts the difficulty of constructing a narrative edifice around loss. Indeed, "To talk" is always "the most difficult." Lyric fragments become a metaphor for the speaker's inability to make meaning from a "scalpel," an "egg," the outline of a beloved "jaw." The sentences themselves often remain unpunctuated, visibly incomplete, and phrased in the conditional. We see that definitive assertion has become yet another impossibility. As Bolden skillfully articulates "an absence, a world," the intervening presence that would provide unity, cohesion, and stability never once appears.

Throughout this collection, lyric address is provocatively emptied of narrative. The result is more real, and more true, than a story ever could be. Rather than recounting to the love object those things that he would more than likely remember ("a strong tooth's gash," "florid school portrait smiles"), he is shown, piece by piece, how he has unmade the world.

With that in mind, *The Sad Epistles* reads as an exploration of desire, power, and disempowerment, the "you" becoming a locus for this loss of voice and agency. As Bolden writes, "This is not simple to say."

Megan Kaminski's *Desiring Map* offers a "you" that is an accumulation of "river," "cloud," and "grass." Yet the "clumps of hills" and "streaming / fields" rarely offer a glimpse of what is already familiar to the love object. Kaminski shows us that to convey desire in language is to create an intricately imagined landscape. The speaker's longing takes shape as a "soft drift" across "the country," "whisps of cold breath" exhaled by someone three cities away. Line by line, she attempts to show the love object a vast expanse, the "rooftops and horizons," he has opened up within her psyche. As in the polyphonic texts of Story, Brimhall, and G'Sell, love is revealed as a seemingly endless topography, rich with sound, echo, and music.

And much like Bolden's artful fragmentation, Kaminski's sonic flourishes read as an extension of content. The music of the poems offers a compelling metaphor for the sublime qualities of the "you." Additionally, Kaminski's mellifluous cadences read as an invitation, a beckoning to the "you" across a widening expanse. "Who can rattle off five addictives / let darkness creep from south," Kaminski writes. Through song, the speaker implores. The assonance in these particular lines (consider the "a" in "can," "rattle," "addictives," the "o" in "off" and "Who") also calls our attention to language as an embodied experience. If spoken aloud, the words become almost tangible, a "ginger gin fizz" in one's mouth. With that in mind, Kaminski draws a clear parallel between language and desire. She calls our attention to the ways that longing, like language, is a bodily experience, a starting ache.

As in Bolden's chapbook, the work of representation is necessitated, and made possible, by distance. The speaker is charged with conveying a loss of beauty, radiance, and possibility in the beloved's absence. Indeed, sublime experience in this collection is almost always past, residing in that "cornflower boundary" the speaker has already traversed. We are borne through memory if only to create music from it.

Purple blossoms bedeck arms
spread down neighborhood trees
I wander in solitude spend hours
calculating the sum of things

Lyric address and its ensuing music become a way of traversing distance, closing the gap between self and other, bringing a distant and inaccessible "you" into closer proximity. Here the "you" is asked to imagine the light, fragrance, and memory that permeate the speaker's surroundings. This intricately imagined landscape, like many others in the book, becomes a kind of shared consciousness, a point of continuity between the always distant "I" and "you," a luminous fiction into which the reader, too, is invited.

SORROW AS DISTANCE AND PROXIMITY: ON SUEYEUN JULIETTE LEE'S *SOLAR MAXIMUM* AND OTHER EXPERIMENTAL TEXTS

At first, the prose paragraphs that comprise Lee's text appear to be presented in an orderly framework, their language as logical as their faultless grammar. As in the poetry of Julia Story and G'Sell, we are led to expect a clear progression between events, a set of causal relationships, an unmistakable narrative arc. Yet Lee inhabits this syntax of well-reasoned exposition while also interrogating it, exploring the "alternative kinetic potentials" residing just beneath this pristine linguistic surface.

"The materials feel good—premium—in your hands," Lee explains. As the book unfolds, she appropriates the tools of conventional meaning-making only to reveal their inherent limitations. We soon realize that the seemingly small distances between each of Lee's sentences will prove difficult, if not impossible, to traverse. The miniscule gaps between her words, the brief silences between utterances, are revealed as cavernous spaces, rife with echoes, containing within them entire metaphysical worlds.

Much like Cohen's fragmented hybrid elegy, Lee subtly and skillfully calls our attention to the ways we attempt to use language, narrative, and the structures of conventional reason to close what we know are impossible distances, to fill the discomfiting silences between words. Indeed, we soon discover that the seemingly compressed linguistic landscape in Solar Maximum does not imply closeness between narrative events, rhetorical modes, or between the text and its reader. Rather, Lee encourages us to consider the infinite varieties (and varying degrees) of distance that permeate what appears at first to be a densely populated narrative framework.

For Lee, literal closeness does not foreclose the possibility of a figurative void. Throughout *Solar Maximum*, the complex and porous relationship between distance and proximity is enacted within the style of the writing itself. Lee's compact yet persistently ruptured syntax enacts these ill-fated attempts to traverse an ever-widening expanse through the generative capabilities of language. In the opening sentences of the book, for example, Lee writes:

Around the Arctic is an imagined circle, and its resolve depends on our shared imagining. We keep it knit there in a version of stasis with our most basic comprehension: our having to triangulate with harsh extremities from vast distances. That circle might now be shrinking or vast quantities of it set loose to fail. Sunblindness is no longer an epiphenomenon.

Lee's syntax, though fulfilling the rules of grammar and its implied causal structures, asks the reader to make leap after thought-provoking logical leap. We are borne from "our own imagining" to the inevitable "failures" of science to the omnipresence of "sunblindness" in a fictive population. What's perhaps most striking about Lee's prose is her conscious choice to eschew the usual transitions, a decision rendered all the more surprising by the smoothness of her syntax. Though the clauses and sentences in *Solar Maximum* fit together neatly, plausibly, and convincingly, the gaps in this conceptually arresting narrative framework are constantly widening.

As readers of *Solar Maximum*, we frequently find ourselves engaged in copious intellectual labor, constructing possible worlds in which Lee's sequential, yet provocatively disparate, sentences cohere. We attempt to create a lovely arc that links each luminous fragment of what seems to be a logical puzzle. Only then do we realize that we have implicated ourselves, as our imaginative work is part of the very cultural machinery that Lee is deconstructing.

"Ultimately, those scarlet engines of speculation. . . lead us into more vigorous wilds," she explains later in the collection. Lee's intentionally permeable narrative conveys, more than anything, a desire for meaning, intentionality, and design where there is none to be found. Given the environmental subject matter of much of the book, which frequently considers the effects of global warming on the physical body, Lee has created a perfect match of form and content. Though our lexicon may be rich, varied, and descriptive, Lee calls our attention to the impossibility of inventing meaning in the case of overt carelessness and reckless disregard.

Our narrative impulses are revealed as futile, even indulgent, in light of the seismic environmental shifts that Lee describes in *Solar Maximum*. As befits an eschewing of the expository capacities of language, the types of rhetorical distance within the text begin to refract and multiply. One inevitably notices that though there is a distinct speaker in these linked poems, with clear voice and unmistakable syntax, the "you" to whom she speaks proves less easy to pinpoint, as the meaning of this seemingly simple pronoun is constantly shifting, proliferating, accumulating.

In many ways, this ambiguity of lyric address also suits Lee's innovative and conceptually arresting elegy for the natural world. Unlike the poetry of Bolden and Kaminski, which counterpoint other types of textual innovation with a remarkable precision of lyric address, Lee embraces hermeneutic uncertainty. In much the same way that the locus of power and agency is persistently dissembled, the "you" becomes increasingly difficult to locate in time, space, and relation to the speaker. The individual(s) being addressed are held at varying degrees of remove from the voice we hear in these intricately linked poems.

At times, we are presented with a general "you," which could be the reader, the narrator herself, or anyone else: "Only you are here." Indeed, this statement could be read as a reflection on the reader's interaction with the text, the impossibility of sharing their imaginative labor and interpretive work as it unfolds. Yet the same passage could be read as a dispatch to a distant though carefully imagined other within the narrative. Approached with these ideas in mind, the particularity of address in other passages proves all the more striking: "It isn't what you asked for, but with it you make do."

Throughout *Solar Maximum*, the increasingly nebulous relationship between the "I" and the "you" serves as a powerful reminder of one's lack of agency as individuals in a larger collective. As an environmental collapse becomes imminent, Lee shows us how the locus of power in this situation is constantly dissembled. As in Cheng's Mao letters, we find that accountability, and the possibility of change, are dislocated, and kept at some degree of remove, through language.

Through this well-reasoned syntax, and the startling narrative ruptures contained therein, Lee offers an innovative and conceptually arresting variation on the traditional elegy. Lee's mourning for the natural world, and the agency of the individual, is gracefully enacted in the silences that permeate her gorgeously fractured prose.

Certainly, the contemporary literary landscape is filled with voices shattered by grief. Christina Davis's *An Ethic*, for example, offers a syntax broken to pieces by loss: "is hard, and therefore a task, to perpetuate / the gesture of welcome" Lines like these, by eschewing the grammatical subject, show us absence by subverting received structures for organizing the world around us. Much like Lee's provocative fragmentation of pure reason, Davis demonstrates through form and technique how grief changes one's existence in language. Within these pristine grammatical constructions, we discover a lack of narrative scaffolding, and as a result, a provocative fragmentation of meaning ideally suited to the book's elegiac subject matter.

Yet Lee offers something entirely new to this ongoing conversation about representing, understanding, and interrogating grief through experiments with form. Lee's poetry is not simply representational, offering a simple mirroring of style and content. Rather, the techniques of poetry are made to do the work of philosophy. She shows us that loss is embedded within language and grammar, that we mourn the distance we cannot traverse through even our most beautiful narrative flourishes. We speak so as not to sense the ruptures contained within our own explanatory narratives,

the absences inscribed before and after each word
on the printed page.

"BLOOD FLOWER": SILENCE & THE UNSPEAKABLE

In *Black Sun*, Julia Kristeva observes that mourning is, in essence, a loss of language. Words abandon their meaning; sentences no longer fit together the way they should. Yet it is language that allows us to derive significance from an experience, integrating it into our understanding of the world around us. The sorrow of a lost object, then, is a double loss: the thing itself has vanished and so too has its place in the lovely arc of story. Once we have fallen out of language, the absence itself becomes unspeakable, and likewise, the stories that make us ourselves.

Three hybrid texts explore, with subtlety and grace, this troubled relationship between grief and the various structures of meaning-making that we have inherited: grammar, narrative, their implied causalities, and their inherent limitations when faced with misfortune. We attempt to impose the logic of story, the clean reasoning of the sentence, when there is no satisfying causal relationship to be found. Allison Benis White's *Please Bury Me in This,* Yanara Friedland's *Uncountry: A Mythology,* and Spring Ulmer's *The Age of Virtual Reproduction* offer a provocative disconnect between their pristine prose paragraphs and the fitting fragmentation of meaning found within them. We are reminded of what it is to be rendered "wordless," with only the "thin clothes" of narrative to cover our grief.

In the work of White, Friedland, and Ulmer, we are made to witness language as it reaches for something that lies just beyond its boundaries. Here, we are offered "glass beads" and "paper houses," "swans" and "paintings of windows" that orbit around an alluringly absent center. The reader is subtly and skillfully implicated in their desire for the story as memento, as "silver, gleaming" keepsake. Yet as sentences begin to assemble themselves in fits and starts, the speakers of these fractured poems are left only with "words, their spectacular lack."

Similar in structure to Emma Bolden's chapbook, White's *Please Bury Me in This* takes the form of prose epistles, in which the terms of address are constantly shifting. In this respect, White's book-length elegy offers a slight departure from *The Wendys*, which proves more explicit in its terms of lyric address. In many ways, the dedication in *Please Bury Me in This* is key to understanding a provocatively destabilized variation on the lyric: *for the four women I knew who took their lives within a year / for my father.* The speaker's grief uncenters her. Voice is revealed as a social construct, predicated on the existence of relationships; without the presence of the other, one struggles to speak. "I want to tell you something memorable,"

White writes, "something you could wear around your neck." Yet this collection does much more, confronting instead the philosophical problems inherent in our desire to memorialize the lost other in language.

As the speaker drifts between remembered scenes, rooms, and objects, the work's neatly constructed prose stanzas prove deceptive, yet purposefully so. As in the poetry of Julia Story, which frequently conjures and undermines readerly expectations, White's justified prose blocks evoke a variety of preconceived ideas readers may have about this particular form: unity of voice, consistency of address, and a readily apparent narrative arc. We have been trained to expect artifice: the "a string of glass beads wrapped several times around" the heroine's neck, "a napkin folded into a swan," then "yet another beautiful thing." Approached with that in mind, the work's fractured, ambulatory structure surprises and delights with its verisimilitude, especially when considering the actual workings of the mind when engulfed by grief:

> And years later, deliriously, when he was dying, Do
> you have the blood flower?
> I was taught to chant 'he loves me, he loves me not' as
> I tore off each petal in my room.
> You are not alone in your feeling of aloneness. Yes, I
> have the blood flower.

White, fittingly and deftly, offers only the illusion

of wholeness. Certainly, the prose in this passage appears in cleanly reasoned sentences, each subject-verb-object construction implying its own discrete causal chain. Yet within this seemingly linear, seemingly rational structure, White skillfully and provocatively fractures time. The "torn petals" and innocent "chant" of the speaker's childhood are held in the mind alongside her later efforts to reach beyond the scope of language and voice: *You are not alone*. This fragmentation of time and narrative, and the layering of discrete temporal moments, calls attention to the artifice of the various frameworks we attempt to impose upon experience. These often linear, often causal ways of creating order from disparate perceptions ultimately fall short of accounting for the ontological violence to which we are all subjected, inevitably. For White, what is truly meaningful resides in the aperture between two words, the threshold between rooms in "the museum of light."

Spring Ulmer's *The Age of Virtual Reproduction* engages similar questions of language and grief, albeit on a larger scale. The work offers a provocative and timely exploration of cultural memory and shared consciousness in the digital age, prompting the reader to consider the changing nature of mourning in a technologized social landscape. Carefully grounded in the writings of Walter Benjamin, August Sander, and John Berger, Ulmer's work provocatively resists the language and structures of theory, seeking instead to create a more personal lexicon for sorrow and the visible fragmentation of culture and community.

Associative in their logic and narrative progression, the linked essays in this collection depict the "fire" and "bullet-shattered glass" of shared mourning while refusing the impulse to weave a master narrative. In many ways, Ulmer's subtle protest, her linguistic resistance, comes across most visibly in the moments of rupture between neatly constructed, seemingly well-reasoned, sentences. Much like White, Ulmer upholds the importance of silence, and the space between words, for deriving meaning from the "played tricks" and "moral . . . anesthesia" that surround us.

She writes in "Peasants":

> They wear suits. Someone once remarked that they do not seem to fit them—their bodies cannot be tailored. I find their unfitted wear beseeching. I want them in these ill-fitting suits, enjoying their outing, looking so ephemeral. It is as if they never stopped for a picture. History cannot remember their names, just their bodies.

As in many passages in *The Age of Virtual Reproduction*, Ulmer's narrator mourns the once clear path to an ethical life. Here the photo, and the perceived innocence of the individuals in "ill-fitting suits," belies the speaker's nostalgia for what she perceived as a less conflicted social landscape. What's perhaps most telling, though, is the rupture between each sentence, the sudden leap from one idea to the next. Though longing for a beautiful past, in which everyone seems at once "beseeching" and charmingly vulnerable, the speaker has internalized the values of the digital age. To move from the suits in the photo to the shortcomings of the human body (which "cannot be tailored") implies a hierarchy, privileging the made thing, the consumer good, over what is human. As in the poetry of Story and G'Sell, Ulmer's swift transitions implicate her own narrator, suggesting that these values no longer warrant justification. In this way, Ulmer's cultural critique, her grief when faced with cultural and political loss, is rendered all the more powerful by the style of her writing. What has been mislaid, for Ulmer, is an ethical sensibility, a moral narrative that once populated the space between actions, the pause between two words.

Much like White and Ulmer, Friedland calls our attention to what's left unsaid, and what cannot be said, in a narrative. *Uncountry: A Mythology* is presented as a series of self-contained flash fictions, which document, in luminous and lyrical fragments, a history of political exile. Often drifting between biblical narratives and twentieth-century politics, Friedland offers a model of time and history that is circular and elliptical. We are pulled again and again towards the same sorrow, a grief that is deeply rooted in a shared cultural memory.

As *Uncountry* progresses, we are made to see that the grief accompanying a lost political struggle, the grief of nationhood, is greater than the individual that bears it. It is a "dark chamber," a "sea" that is constantly widening within the individual psyche. Friedland writes, for example, in "History of Breath":

> Above the fireplace, which is never lit, his face during wartime. Full uniform, legs crossed, face in half profile against a wall of windows. On the table next to him a plant, cup saucer, a hunched angel in bronze.

What's perhaps most telling about this passage is its purposeful ambiguity. We are presented with archetypes of a mythic quality—the "half profile" of the soldier in "full uniform, legs crossed," the "hunched angel in bronze." In much the same way that Friedland forgoes specificity in description, so too the narrative drifts between wars and exiles, which slowly accumulate, one superimposed over the other. In many ways, it is this refusal of singularity that is one of the most powerful techniques that Friedland has at her disposal. By unsaying the particular, and denying the purported uniqueness of each sorrow, she gestures toward the presence of a larger cultural machine, which ceaselessly replicates archetypes, myths, mistakes.

Much like White's gorgeously elusive prose, and Ulmer's wild associative leaps, Friedland's stately and mythic micro-narratives are perhaps most powerful in their silences. She reminds us to examine the space between words, the ethical implications of all what cannot, and will not, be said.

If mourning is a loss of language and narrative, perhaps that silence can be brought to bear on its own provocation. In the work of White, Ulmer, and Friedland, mourning, and its accompanying quiet, is no longer a passive endeavor. Rather, one's alienation from language, its implied order and structure, becomes pure possibility, a source of transformation, wonder, and insight.

Their work shows us that silence can be made to speak on behalf of the lost other, perhaps even more powerfully than the familiar and ready-made structures of narrative. In each, we are made to witness the underlying logic and assumptions of language as they are unsaid, and in this unsaying, we see them, suddenly, finally, and irrevocably, anew.

AN AFTERWORD

NOLI ME TANGERE: NOTES ON LANGUAGE & VIOLENCE

As a student, I was obedient. I rarely questioned anyone who spoke with the least bit of authority. Yet the whole time, I remember an unease blossoming beneath my skin. Its petals unfurling one by one as the pages of my manuscript were turned by my classmates.

I cannot seem to enter the text. The text isn't granting me access.
Why can't I enter the text.

At the time of the critique, I had been keenly interested in exploring textual difficulty as a feminist gesture. By then twenty-eight years old, I spent several years bouncing back and forth between various low-residency MFA programs, artist colonies, and noncredit workshops, searching for a sense of artistic community. No matter what landscape, building, or campus, I remained deeply disturbed by one thing: the difficult text was almost always spoken about as though it were a female body, and as though the primarily male readers in the room were entitled to "access" it.

This mindset—the belief that every artistic work should yield to the hand of a reader who attends closely enough to syntax, his pocket Lacan dictionary at arm's reach—was, in my estimation, deeply symptomatic. In recent years, the reading act has ceased to be an exercise in humility but has instead been transfigured into a visible wielding of mastery, a desire to dominate and colonize.

As Teresa D. Lauretis observes in her study of gender and reading practices, "French feminism goes as far as to consider the act of interpretation a patriarchal enterprise, the goal of which is to achieve power or mastery over a given text. In this theoretical schema, the text is identified with femininity, and interpretation becomes a way of arresting the free play of meaning analogous to the way patriarchy contains women and women's sexuality."

In so many of these classroom discussions, the text is made to stand in for the female body, and all the violence that is suffered by female bodies, here, is done again through language, through interpretation, and through the orders of power that undergird the settings in which this feedback is given.

*

Of course, many of the poems I submitted for the requisite critiques intentionally violated readerly expectations. I reacted against the abiding belief that as a younger female writer, I was expected to give a certain amount of emotion, not more, not less.

In her book *The End of the Sentimental Journey*, Sarah Vap describes the fraught relationship between the reading act and what she calls "a payoff." According to Vap, readers need a text to be "just easy enough." That is, readers generally like to feel as though the text has given into them, but also, they like to feel that they've worked for it. She situates textual difficulty and easiness on a spectrum, asking the reader to find the sweet spot.

Certainly, Vap calls our attention to the similarities in how textual bodies and physical bodies are constructed in language. The challenge to us as her audience, then, was to exist beyond or outside of this conversation. To forge a new vocabulary, a new syntax, a lexicon that's more hospitable to innovation by women.

For me, this feminist utopia had already become a republic of one.

*

We tend to forget that the workshop model of creative writing instruction is predicated on disenfranchisement. We watch as others attempt to gain visible mastery over our voices, our aesthetic predilections, our lives in language, and in most pedagogical settings, we are not allowed to interject. For individuals who come from a demographic in society that has been silenced, denied, or disempowered in some way, the workshop model often appears as yet another manifestation of power and violence.

The only good writer in a workshop is a dead writer. You are a dead writer starting NOW. . . .

In a recent essay, Viet Thanh Ngugen notes that "Literature and power cannot be separated. American literature is read around the world not only because of its inherent value, but because the rest of the world always reads the literature of empires." The workshop model of instruction often functions as an extension of empire, facilitated by those who have vested stakes in the current orders of power.

Yes, of course, graduate students need to learn how to receive constructive feedback gracefully, to listen, and speak only when it is their turn. But the usual workshop pedagogy affects different types of artistic practitioners in dissimilar, often incommensurable, ways. It is perhaps most problematic for a writer working outside of legible and familiar forms, attempting to effect social change through the very foundations of society: language itself.

As an experimental feminist practitioner, I often felt as though I were staring the status quo in the face during my class critiques. After all, nearly ninety percent of full-time faculty in such settings are white, and well over seventy percent are white men.

*

WORKSHOP VIOLENCE:
A PARTIAL ARCHIVE

"The speaker of the poem is not a likeable girl."

"No. You have to understand. Kristina chose this found language and the fact that she chose it, well, this says something about her."

"Kristina's poems are an insult to her accomplished collaborator's intelligence."

"I don't understand why Kristina writes in broken forms. Maybe this means she was the victim of sexual violence at some point."

"Writing a feminist response to Shakespeare is elitist. And classist. I mean, you have to have gone to a college and read *Hamlet* to get the poem."

"Who cares."

"Actually..."

"I think the poem is *about*..."

*

In my nearly ten years in graduate school, what disturbed me most about workshops were the moments in which the writing served as merely a vehicle, a vast storehouse of language from which men (and sometimes women) could craft pickup lines. Textual and bodily conquest were indelibly linked for many aspiring and mid-career practitioners.

A recent survey found that 38% of female respondents in graduate programs have been sexually harassed by men in a position of authority over their academics. The percentage that includes harassment by male peers is much larger.

I haven't heard from you in a couple of months, Kristina. Now tell me whether or not you've had sex with him.

I enrolled in my first workshop because I aspired to better journal publications. Instead, I was surveilled by male poets via the internet, and by their departmental secretaries when they did not have time to surveil me themselves. I witnessed frustrated desire exorcised onto my poems, which in turn became sites of various male poets' catharsis. My poems also served as a mere opportunity for various abuses of power.

You and I should work on a collaboration, Kristina. I think a good first step would be you buying a plane ticket and flying here to have sex with me.

When I mentioned this exchange to my friend, she looked at me and said, "You are clearly just the girl in this batch of girls. Next year there will be a fresh batch."

*

In late 2012, I was the victim of an attempted assault by my instructor's colleague. He switched my drink at a party, but I wouldn't drink it. In the months that followed, I changed my phone number. Still, he sent me the most terrifying things in the mail.

Needless to say, my writing workshopmates were bludgeoned with angry story after angry story, all of them about young women who looked like me, and who were eventually found dead in the woods.

The class critiques quickly turned into a trial, and my ability as the star witness was called into question:

The language is not compelling when you write about the violence men have done to you.
I don't understand why you would have chosen that dress at all.
No, no, this work is not on the same level as your poems to him about love.

When violence could no longer be enacted on my physical body, the text was again proffered as a substitute, standing in as the object of male aggression.

With that said, I never took my evals. I did not want an institutional record of my trauma because I did not want to see it redacted, written over, or erased.

ACKNOWLEDGEMENTS

Thank you to the editors of the following magazines, where early versions of these essays first appeared:

The *American Poetry Review* (APR), *Gulf Coast, Ploughshares, Poetry International,* the *Los Angeles Review of Books,* the *Iowa Review,* the *Brooklyn Rail, Tarpaulin Sky*, and the *Literary Review*.

Thank you to The American Academy in Rome, Yaddo, The Helene Wurlitzer Foundation, and 360 Xochi Quetzal, where early drafts of these essays were written. Thank you as well to C&R Press, who printed earlier versions of a few of these essays in chapbook form.

This book is for my teachers and my family.